ENTANGLEMENTS

New ecopoetry

edited by
David Knowles and Sharon Blackie

TWO RAVENS PRESS

Published by Two Ravens Press Ltd.
Taigh nam Fitheach
26 Breanish, Uig
Isle of Lewis HS2 9HB
United Kingdom

www.tworavenspress.com

The right of the editors and contributors to be identified as authors of their work included in this volume has been asserted by them in accordance with the Copyright, Designs & Patent Act, 1988.
Anthology © Two Ravens Press, 2012.
The copyright of individual poems and texts remains with their authors.

ISBN: 978-1-906120-65-8

British Library Cataloguing in Publication Data: a CIP record for this book can be obtained from the British Library.

All rights reserved. No part of this publication may be reproduced, stored in a retrieval system, or transmitted in any other form or by any means, electronic, mechanical, photocopying, recording or otherwise without the prior written permission of the publishers. This book may not be lent, hired out, resold or otherwise disposed of by way of trade in any form of binding or cover other than that in which it is published, without the prior consent of the publishers.

Designed and typeset in Sabon by Two Ravens Press.

Printed in Poland on
Forest Stewardship Council-accredited paper.

Front cover artwork: Douglas Robertson
www.douglasrobertson.co.uk

About the Editors

Sharon Blackie and David Knowles founded independent literary publisher Two Ravens Press in 2006, and *EarthLines* Magazine (for writing about nature, place and the environment) in 2012. Sharon's critically acclaimed first novel was *The Long Delirious Burning Blue* (2008); she is now editor of *EarthLines*. David's first poetry collection *Meeting the Jet Man* was shortlisted for the 2009 Scottish Arts Council First Book of the Year award, and a poem from it was Highly Commended in the 2010 Forward Prize.

David and Sharon run *EarthLines* and Two Ravens Press from their working croft by the sea, right at the end of the most south-westerly road on the Isle of Lewis in the Outer Hebrides. *Taigh nam Fitheach* (House of the Ravens) is home to Hebridean and Jacob sheep, two breeding sows, a Kerry milk cow, bees, a miscellany of poultry, and a polytunnel.

For more information, see:

www.tworavenspress.com

www.earthlines.org.uk

Contents

Editors' Notes	XI
Introduction by Dr. David Borthwick	XV

Catherine Owen

Nature Writing 101	1
Beseech	2
They Will Disappear These Ruins & This Beauty Too	3

John Kinsella

Sundews and 'Enzymatic Absorption' Versus All Flesh-Feeding Plants Anyway	4
Penillion of Stanbury Moor: 'There shines the moon, at noon of night –'	5
Penillion of Cambridgeshire as My Body	6

Jim Carruth

Because the Land Are We	8
Mapping	9
Legacy	10

Meg Bateman

Touched	11

Dilys Rose

Stone the Crows	12

Andy Brown

Nocturne	13
Pen y Fan	14
The Wood for the Trees	15

Isabel Galleymore

Silvics	16
Harvest	17
Curculio	17

Jos Smith
                    Witness   18

Ben Smith
                    from Lessons in Augury   19

Terry Jones
                    Economies   22
                    Awkward Bird   23
                    Bee   24

Chris McCully
                    Watching White-trout on the River Dargle
                                                        25

Gerry Loose
                    from Fault Line   26

Susan Rowland
                    For the Forest   35
                    What the Trees Want   36
                    Run Your Hands…   37

Sharon Black
                    Dharma   38
                    Fingal's Cave   39

Charles Wilkinson
                    from The Marches   40
                    The Happiness Over the Hill   42

Ariel Gordon
                    Semioviparous   43
                    How to Survive in the Woods   45
                    How to Water Your Lawn Effectively   46

David Troupes
                    from God of Corn   47

Arpine Konyalian Grenier
                    If not, Winter   51
                    Hit by Her Ancient Wings   52
                    Flatly Present my Shame   55

Howard Giskin
        Mountain Lion Tracks   57
        Pine Barrens   58

Rupert M Loydell
        Bright Currency   59
        Apples, Storm, Adventure   60

Alec Finlay
        wind-songs   61

John Glenday
        Only a leaf for a sail   64
        Allt Dearg   64
        Birch Wind   65

Jorie Graham
        Of Inner Experience   66
        The Bird That Begins It   70
        Earth   75

Gordon McInnes
        Held and Held in Place   82
        Slem   83

Mark Goodwin
        Pity & Wild   85

Mario Petrucci
        close in in   88
        when milk enters   89

Ian Seed
        Senza Risposta   91

Allen Tullos
        Data Points Cloud the Event Horizon   92

Cathleen Allyn Conway
        The Pageant   93

Jane Joritz-Nakagawa
        The Lighthouse   94
        The End of History   95

Elizabeth Dodd
>   Panic   96
>   The Problem of Moral Relevance Blooms
>   on North Mesa   97

Andrew Forster
>   The Duddon Valley   98

C. J. Allen
>   Abandoned Millstones   99
>   Wooden Boulder   100

Frances Presley
>   Oak Change   102

Pippa Little
>   Belnahua   104

Ruth Padel
>   Meeting the Lemming   105

Em Strang
>   The Woodchester Beast   106
>   The Place   107
>   Parsnip   108

Jennifer Wallace
>   My Eyes Look Everywhere: Needles and
>   Neon, a Few Squirrels   110
>   I wanted to change my name   111

Fiona Russell
>   At the Old Buchts   112
>   Dod Fell   113
>   Wee Byre, After the Storm   114

Roger Mitchell
>   Undersong   115
>   In a Field   117

Paul Lindholdt
>   Brooding Season   119

Alistair Peebles
        Provided   120
        Heather linties, hundreds   121
        And so   125

dee Hobsbawn-Smith
        Driving the Mares   127
        Hejira   128
        Flood Plain   130

Rody Gorman
        Air an Doirling mu Dheireadh   132
        On the Last Pebblygulfstreampeninsulasound
        at Last   133

Susie Patlove
        Divertimento   134

David Chorlton
        What Comes   136
        Wolf Politics   138

Les Murray
        High Speed Trap Space   139

Paul Kingsnorth
        The Testament of Edward Abbey   140
        From the Fjord   141

Jane Routh
        The Teachings of *Strix aluco*   142
        The Private Life of *Lepus lepus*   143
        Mark-making   146

Kathleen Jones
        Raven Goes Travelling   147
        The Islands of the Light   150
        The Hunters   151

Susan Richardson
        The White Doe   152

Jane McKie
    THE RIFE   154
    BEACHING OF A POD OF WHALES AT LOCH CARNAN
    154

Nancy Holmes
    SUBURBAN SUMMER ODE   155
    THE SPIRIT OF RESISTANCE   157

Mark Tredinnick
    OWLS   159
    DRESS REHEARSAL   160
    READING THE GITA AGAIN IN EARLY SPRING   161

Katrina Porteous
    THE WHALE   163

Alice Oswald
    SHARPHAM HOUSE   164

CONTRIBUTORS   173

Editors' Notes

The animal that is poetry thrives when under pressure, when stressed. It grows lithe and fit. It no longer frets and scratches at its own skin. As Ruth Padel noted[1], the achievements of poetry under the oppressive regimes of the Soviet Union and the quality of writing springing from the Troubles in Ireland were no chance occurrences – this was poetry rising to a challenge. The ecological catastrophe we face at the beginning of the twenty-first century is neither an oppressive political regime *per se*, nor is it what is conventionally meant by violence. Yet many poets have for a long time felt the pressure of pollution or habitat loss or species extinction or climate change in the background of their work. For some, such as Wendell Berry or Ted Hughes, the spectre of ecological destruction is a constant, goading presence. For many others it has been a half-conscious nightmare, stalking them at the margins of daily life.

The bad dreams are now the daily newspaper headlines. What once was a dull pervasive ache is now an ever-more-frequent acute stabbing pain. It seemed to us that the whole poetry animal, from the sonnet to the Open Field, the prose poem to the ballad, had turned to face head-on our increasingly problematic relationship with the nonhuman world. This was the context in which we decided to bring together this anthology.

As we face up to the reality of climate change and the likelihood of irreversible damage to the biosphere, we are frequently called to alter our behaviour and lifestyles, to revisit our relationship with the environment and, somehow, to 'reconnect with nature'. But what does reconnection mean, and, more importantly, what does it imply about how we live? Is it always warm and cosy, or are there less comfortable aspects

---

[1] Introduction to *52 Ways of Looking at a Poem*, Vintage (2002)

to that connection? And does literature, and specifically poetry, have any role to play in our reconnection? Can a poem help bridge the growing dissociation that pervades the relationships between contemporary humans and the natural world? These are the issues that we wanted to explore in *Entanglements*.

We chose to produce an anthology of *new* ecopoetry that reflects this specific time of transition: the transition from a world in which global ecological damage is just one issue amongst many, to a world in which our species' relationship with the global ecosystem is *the* issue. We are attempting to take a snapshot of poetic output as humans and the planet stand at a crossroads. And in this sense, *Entanglements* differs from previous excellent anthologies which have provided a broad overview of ecopoetry over the centuries – of which a list is provided on page xxi.

We received a very large number of submissions for *Entanglements*, and faced many difficult choices when making our selections. We ruled out poems that were largely political, or straightforwardly 'environmental' poems, because we had called for something different: for a new wave of poetry that seeks to directly respond to the world in which we find ourselves, and that dramatises a growing hunger for a meaningful connection with the earth.

Among such poems we received many which expressed a deep optimism, and others which bore a profound pessimism. There was joy in the natural world, and anguish at its ongoing and inexorable destruction. There was anger at what other people were doing to the planet, and there was guilt about how 'I' relate to the earth. We have tried to reflect the breadth and complexity of all of these responses, as well as the different forms in which they were presented. In many of the poems we selected, opposing emotions were forced to confront each other – with powerful results. Many of the poems present novel, local or perhaps just forgotten ways of relating to the world around us. We had called for poetry written in English, but in this context it is worth saying a few words about the inclusion of a poem in Gaelic by Rody Gorman, alongside its transposition into English. The extent to which the very different language that is Gaelic allows the speaker to inhabit a place differently – allows a different way of experiencing the natural world – can be tantalisingly glimpsed in the poem's English echo. This poem and many others in *Entanglements* function as signposts and waymarkers – though we must ourselves still tramp the long road to which they point.

The ordering of the poems is loose, and went through so many iterations that at one point we likened the task to deciding the best order in which to load Noah's Ark. The very first poem and the last remained where they are throughout all the changes, but most of the other poems have had different neighbours at some point. There is no perfect order for such a wide-ranging collection of poems, but our challenge was to avoid any ghettos of form or of viewpoint. We have attempted to present a dappled light, an actual entanglement of conflicting emotions and methods of expression. For Garrett Hardin's first law of human ecology states that everything is interconnected, and it is in this spirit that we offer you *Entanglements*.

We would like to thank the poets, all of whom have allowed their work to be used for no personal gain, since royalties will be donated to The John Muir Trust *(www.jmt.org)* an organisation that fights hard and well to protect wild land in a world in which it is constantly under threat. We would like particularly to thank Dr David Borthwick of the University of Glasgow for his enthusiasm, encouragement, and moral and practical support, extending to the very fine introduction on the following pages.

David Knowles & Sharon Blackie
Taigh nam Fitheach, Isle of Lewis, July 2012

Introduction

Dr. David Borthwick, University of Glasgow

The poems gathered here come under the title *Entanglements*. Entanglement suggests ensnarement in briars, or brambles; but equally barbed wire. An entanglement describes the sinuous weaves of electric flex that power the technology we're plugged into. Complex family relationships are a secure net in which we are – if we are lucky – enmeshed, an entanglement of roots. Place and community, site and city, provide entanglements: in geology, topography, ecology, memory and tradition. Television and the internet, world travel and global commodities, find us entangled in ever greater lines of communication and consumption.

There is no escaping entanglements, and ways of describing the ecological relationship between humans and the world they share with non-human species are myriad, from the classical Great Chain of Being to Robert Kirk's universe in his *Secret Commonwealth* of 1691, which ordered the inhabitants of the earth according to the altitudes they occupied, 'Manucodiata, or Bird of Paradise' being closest to heaven, with 'Worms, Otters, Badgers' and fish being closest to hell. Humans and 'Beasts', it is worth noting, are but one region beyond. More recent ideas of humankind's place in the world, its connection to the earth, are less hierarchical, recognising that the lines between human and nonhuman are less defined, not linear chains or tidy strata, but more messy, less coherent: there is no 'natural world' that does not also include humans. Nature is not on another planet. Denise Levertov famously described the 'great web' of ecology, stressing the connection of all things, 'designed, beyond / all spiderly contrivance, / to link, not to entrap.' Introducing

Wild Reckoning, a collection of poems 'provoked' by *Silent Spring*, John Burnside and Maurice Riordan assert that what Rachel Carson wanted to show us was 'not that everything was interconnected, as in some web or lattice ... but that matter is continuous, like a Celtic knot.' Knots. Webs. Entanglements.

The central concern of ecopoetry is recognition of human entanglement in the world. It explores the relationships that humans have with a shared world, at once connected to it but also increasingly estranged from it. Ecopoetry seeks to question and renegotiate the human position in respect of the environment in which we are enmeshed. Its ethic is to oppose the violent assumption that the world around us exists merely as a set of resources which can be readily and unethically exploited and degraded for economic gain. We are arguably in a new geological epoch, the anthropocene, in which the human impact on the earth's ecosystems is such that the regulatory dynamics of the earth are influenced disproportionately, dangerously, by human activity. 'What's most in need of re-negotiation and repair,' Kathleen Jamie has said, 'is our relationship with the natural world. We're learning, or re-learning, that this is the only world, it's not an anteroom or preparation for something "better." Neither is it an infinite "resource."'

Ecopoems signal a conscious re-engagement with a world that is familiar and strange, full of animals and plants that we must answer to, and which we need to address, again, more carefully, to define the questions that will help us to negotiate ways of living in an uncertain future of biodiversity loss, climate change and the consequences of disposability. As Laurence Buell pointed out in the mid-1990s, 'environmental crisis involves a crisis of the imagination the amelioration of which depends on finding better ways of imagining nature and humanity's relation to it.' It is out of this will to re-imagine, re-engage, that the term ecopoetry was born, finding expression in the early twenty-first century in work by Jonathan Bate, among others, whose seminal

The Song of the Earth (2000) defined ecopoetry with reference to etymology: 'Ecopoetics asks in what respects a poem may be a making (Greek *poiesis*) of the dwelling-place – the prefix eco- is derived from Greek *oikos*, "the home or place of dwelling."' Jonathan Skinner's influential US magazine *Ecopoetry* used its first issue in 2001 to describe how '"*Eco*" here signals—no more, no less—the home we share with several million other species, our planet Earth. "*Poesis*" is used as *poesis* or making... Thus ecopoetics: a house making.' Ecopoetry, then, as a putting of one's house in order; or a re-building of it, recognising that the previous configurations of one's imagined place in the *oikos* – the place of our common dwelling in the world, our original habitat – were dysfunctional, destructive. But Harriet Tarlo has objected to this definition, pointing out that 'house making' is 'uncomfortably domestic' and seems to retain an emphasis on 'the human's residence on earth as the centre of the universe.'

Leonard Scigaj, writing in 1999, called for 'a poetry that treats nature as a separate and equal other and includes respect for nature conceived as a series of ecosystems—dynamic and potentially self-regulating cyclic feedback systems.' He described the need for a poetry emphasising equality, while also under no illusion that ecosystems persist, on the whole, without, or despite, human interference or concern. Yet John Kinsella is not convinced that such a poetry is possible, pointing out that 'as long as one engages with the materials of human "progress", there is no way that a reality of "equal other" exists... The privileged can never account for themselves as an equal other.'

Ecopoetry cannot avoid the human 'I' at its centre: the observer, the speaker, the human voice communicating. What it can do, however, is to strive to represent relationships with the environment, to be scrupulous in its observance of the condition of enmeshment in the world. John Burnside has expressed this impulse succinctly: 'I consider the animal and plant life around me, not as metaphors, or emblems, but as living forms with whom I would discover a continuity... I am interested in a world that extends beyond human preferences to "everything that is the case."'

Many of the ecopoems gathered here concern such attempts at 'connection,' a re-evaluation of human status in potent moments of heightened observation, sensory immersion. Jonathan Bate gives a somewhat romantic account of this process, describing how 'reverie, solitude, walking' are essential; he says: 'to turn these experiences into language is to be an ecopoet. Ecopoetry is not a description of dwelling with the earth, not a disengaged thinking about it, but an experiencing of it.' This immersive brand of verse uses sensory experience, embodied practice, as a means of articulating questions, an internal re-calibration of the relationship between the self and the nonhuman others with whom the environment is shared.

Ecopoetry can also be more directly political, however, addressing particular examples of environmental damage, or engaging with the patterns of thought and behaviour that permit rapacious consumption. Neil Astley's introduction to his collection *Earth Shattering* (2007) defines ecopoetry in terms of its ability to 'dramatise the dangers and poverty of a modern world perilously cut off from nature and ruled by technology, self-interest and economic power.' While some critics have questioned whether it is poetry's job to be so overtly political, it is a poet's right to respond to compelling issues as they see fit, and the issues to which such poets speak are of such urgency that formal definitions of how poetry *ought* to behave seem counter-productive. Indeed, there are poems in this collection which bear similar sentiments to those of William Wordsworth, whose poem in the autumn of 1844 protested against the 'rash assault' upon the landscape of the projected Kendal and Windermere railway.

Ecopoetry, then, is not a prescriptive definition, but instead acknowledges a responsiveness to, a responsibility for, a shared environment at a crucial moment when the polar twins of human history and 'natural history' are melting, intermingling in the flow of unpredictable events and consequences, present and yet-to-come. Laura-Gray Street and Ann Fisher-Wirth describe a 'shifting, intermingling landscape' of ecopoetry, 'in which all forms have bearing and legitimacy, their presences and purposes ebbing and flowing ... at different times and in different communities and contexts.'

Many of the poems in this collection have specific places at their heart, sharing with Wendell Berry the conviction that 'to have a place, to live and belong in a place, to live from a place without destroying it, we must imagine it.' Place offers a solace and grounding for many ecopoets, a site for digging in, gaining insights from which to see a wider connection to a shared world. Others take a more global view, wrestling with wider perspectives and other kinds of connection, strands of web: the way in which global issues are here, in the place we inhabit, brought to us in the goods we purchase, the information we consume, the knowledge we cannot ignore: that the local is the global, too.

The poems collected here take many forms, from hymns and laments to dirges and panegyrics; contemplative moments to narratives of transformation, immersion and hope. There is anger, struggle and clear-eyed engagement; there is memory, myth and despair. These poets wrestle with the disorientating nature of environmental issues, a reminder that entanglement also means complication, confusion, lacking means of extrication. Environmental issues are so bewildering because of their diversity and number. The environmental question is not something. It is everything. The dizzying character of global concerns has been captured in a new metaphor, coined by Tim Morton in his book *The Ecological Thought* (2010). In it, he discusses the global 'mesh' that humans inhabit, describing how the connectedness of all things can destabilise our ability to see clearly. Morton puts it like this: 'since everything is interconnected, there is no definite background and therefore no definite foreground.' We are hopelessly entangled in global environmental issues, each one connected, at once distant and close at hand, animal extinction to water pollution, global weirding to hydraulic fracking, plastic waste to wind turbines, washing powder to bottom trawling. Perhaps this is why place becomes so important to many ecopoets. Amid this vertigo-inducing range of global threats, one must first find where one stands.

There can be no denying, though, that where many ecopoets stand is in the 'developed' world. Ecopoetry is at present a predominantly western movement, emanating from writers who take their responsibility seriously to stand against the myths of domination and disposability that characterise, but also emanate from, the places they stand in. There is no room for piety, however, instead a profound need for honesty: the poets here, primarily from the UK, the USA, Canada, and Australia, find their voices more readily heard owing to the circumstances which progress has permitted. But there must be room for critique, for reckoning; room for imagination as agitation, space for a poetics of commitment.

Ecopoetry is a subtle form of activism. Poetry is not perhaps the most obvious means of reaching a wide audience in the twenty-first century. But it is a vital form which retains health even in its contemporary marginality. And this is what makes poetry so crucial, being one of the few forms it is difficult to make conform to corporate utility, its fundamental features acknowledging complexity and the difficulty of expression, rather than endorsing simplicity, instant apprehension, the superficially clear yet disposable soundbite. Poetry's notorious instability of meaning, its protean shifting, its rhythmic soundings, resist swift dismissal. Poetry is a terrestrial channel in a digital age, grounded and grounding, set firmly in the soil of the real.

I have avoided any mention of this as an anthology of ecopoems, and quite deliberately. An anthology – as the *antho-*prefix reveals – is a collection of flowers, a garden of verse, or perhaps a vase: a vessel filled with poor, rarefied specimens. Something else is needed here. Sticking with the entangling nature of the poems, perhaps the cosmopolitan genus *rubus* might provide a more fitting description. The flowering plants of the *rubus* genus include the raspberry and the bramble; their fruit is many-faceted, an aggregate sequence of patterns ('drupelets'). Their sinuous canes send out recurved thorns, designed to ensnare, not to let one go easily. This seems fitting, and so I will use it. *Entanglements* is a rubusology of ecopoems.

Further Reading

Anthologies

Peter Abbs, *Earth Songs: A Resurgence Anthology of Contemporary Ecopoetry* (Totnes: Green Books, 2002).

Madhur Anand and Adam Dickinson, eds., *Regreen: New Canadian Ecological Poetry* (Sudbury, Ontario: Your Scrivener Press, 2009).

Neil Astley, ed., *Earth Shattering: Ecopoems* (Tarset, Northumberland: Bloodaxe, 2007).

John Burnside and Maurice Riordan, eds., *Wild Reckoning: An Anthology Provoked by Rachel Carson's Silent Spring* (London: Calouste Gulbenkian Foundation, 2004).

Sara Dunn and Alan Scholefield, eds., B*eneath the Wide Wide Heaven: Poetry of the Environment from Antiquity to the Present* (London: Virago, 1991).

Ann Fisher-Wirth and Laura-Gray Street, eds., *The Ecopoetry Anthology* (San Antonio, TX: Trinity University Press, 2013).

Alice Oswald, ed., *The Thunder Mutters: 101 Poems for the Planet* (London: Faber, 2005).

Harriet Tarlo, ed., *The Ground Aslant: An Anthology of Radical Landscape Poetry* (Exeter: Shearsman Books, 2011).

Criticism

Jonathan Bate, *The Song of the Earth* (London: Picador, 2000).

J. Scott Bryson, *Ecopoetry: A Critical Introduction* (Salt Lake City: University of Utah Press, 2002).

Timothy Clark, *The Cambridge Introduction to Literature and the Environment* (Cambridge: Cambridge University Press, 2011).

James Engelhardt, 'The Language Habitat: An Ecopoetry Manifesto,' *Octopus Magazine*, Issue 9, http://www.octopusmagazine.com/Issue09/engelhardt.html

John Felsteiner, *Can Poetry Save the Earth? A Field Guide to Nature Poems* (New Haven: Yale University Press, 2009).

Terry Gifford, *Green Voices: Understanding Contemporary Nature Poetry*, 2nd Edition (Nottingham: Critical, Cultural and Communications Press, 2011).

John Kinsella, *Activist Poetics: Anarchy in the Avon Valley*, ed. Niall Lucy (Liverpool: Liverpool University Press, 2010).

Helen Moore, 'What is Ecopoetry?', *International Times*, http://internationaltimes.it/what-is-ecopoetry/

Timothy Morton, *The Ecological Thought* (Cambridge, Mass.: Harvard University Press, 2010).

Leonard M. Scigaj, *Sustainable Poetry: Four American Ecopoets* (Lexington, Kentucky: University Press of Kentucky, 1999).

Laura-Gray Street and Ann Fisher-Wirth, 'Ecopoetry,' *Verse Wisconsin*, 107 (November 2011), http://www.versewisconsin.org/Issue107/prose/gray_fisher-wirth.html

Harriet Tarlo, 'Women and Ecopoetics: An Introduction in Context,' *How2*, Vol. 3, No. 2 (Summer 2008), http://www.asu.edu/pipercwcenter/how2journal/vol_3_no_2/ecopoetics/introstatements/tarlo_intro.html

Ecopoetics, influential US periodical edited by Jonathan Skinner. Full-text back issues can be downloaded at http://ecopoetics.wordpress.com/

Catherine Owen

Nature Writing 101

Our minds can turn anything romantic.
Is the problem.
The sewagy mud of the Fraser a quaint muslin & the spumes

    pulsing out of chimneys at the Lafarge cement plant look,
    at night, like two of Isadora Duncan's scarves, pale,
                                insouciant veils,
    harmless. The trees are all gone but then aren't our hearts

more similar to wastelands.
We can make it kin, this pollution, children one is sad about
                            yet still fond of, their
delinquency linked to our own, irreparable with familiarity,
                    a lineage of stench &

    forgiveness. Our minds can assimilate all horrors.
    Is the problem.
    The animals will disappear and those small,
                          strange invertebrates,

the bees will vanish & in the well-oiled waters, fish
will surge their deaths over the sand bags.
But then we keep saying, 'Let's construct another narrative.'

    The nightmares must simply be called reality.
    And after this you see,
    it is possible to carry on.

Beseech

Prolong me along the estuary
    where the cataclysmic wildflowers, all their
                      poppy-joy-vermilion
smitten in pointillist manifold burgeon
   & there are discarded rust hungers too beautiful to not be
un-wedged from granite and shouldered home,
                    such bolts & rivets of ruin
    have we here below the swallow tidbit draughts
                      of slight salt water
& slim oil from the tug-lovely voyages, green peeling barges,
                        power boats
    and the occasional Sea-Doo though the fishing lines
                      continue to fall
from the small dreams of wharves while toddlers
                  bucket & cry on shorelines
    passed by the endless joggers. O prolong me along
                  the estuary there
is something in this thin stretch of eel grass & bulrushes
              where the tide skew-wiffs in
    against the slow-eroding boardwalk that is hope-solemn,
                  proven re-tuning
of what has been somewhat death-struck-numb and now wants,
              if living is what it does,
    to be vole-slickery and gold-holy as those dandelions tall
                  beside the Fraser
and of their origins, stone, perhaps, or song.

They Will Disappear These Ruins & This Beauty Too

They will disappear these ruins & this beauty too & this
                            indistinguishable – I just wanted
    a raw place to wander in and for them also, a random spot
                            – you can't find

anything in townhouses & skyscrapers – O manicured
                           & upright dwellings – there are no
    blackberries here, no sandpipers, no bull frogs,
                      no swallows' nests, no dead lobsters, no

rotting fish, no old ropes or any other signs of history to
                           speak of in copper or brick or steel
    or flesh – we are afraid for the children always –
                    in this last undeveloped zone on earth

where the final species breathe – it is not enough
                to have everything – nothing will soon be ours
    & the ads singing haven over the barren inhabited lands
                           will show glorious faces,

glossy hands, bright feet – these will move down the sharp
                    delineated paths – these will not stop
    to feel – the empty river groomed for them as wallpaper,
                           as screen – its mind only

waiting for our absence.

John Kinsella

Sundews and 'Enzymatic Absorption' Versus All Flesh-Feeding Plants Anyway

Sticky about heels moving fast through damp
bush and swampland, a delicate tangle, more
unsettling for fixing dead or struggling ants
which will haunt with formic mapping,
countless lives strung up, threads to hold
a bobbin on its spool, allurer or speculator,
apocryphal or portentous, a tearing away
before the science took hold and guilt
declared 'Carnivorous'. Self-fascination:
and then a silence, a survival post-contact
just a case of scale: to break down
into cries and pleas, the gasps
absorbed into the vegetal world:
glistening in sun before it goes under,
a new scale offered for comprehension's
sake; take black holes: categories
increasing as stars shine bright
on the edge of gravity: miniatures,
stellar, supermassive. A necklace
of cupped coffins winking, the end
of all life declaring beauty which rests
in the plant eating the animal:
which it does, which it always does.

Penillion of Stanbury Moor: 'There shines the moon, at noon of night – '

Segmentation
Of field – flection
Of plastic bound
Bales; that moss-stoned

Vista across
The weir & gross
Wind twisting wool
And feathers all

Across the moors,
Into water's
Skin: some boat here
Through the summer,

Restrained narrow
Cleft, inland show
Of valley flight,
Floored millstone grit

And glib thorn trees
Sense ring ouzels
Vindicating
Their rights; nearing.

Penillion of Cambridgeshire as My Body

Those chronicles
And spectacles
Of reeds, sedges,
Rushes ... hedges.

Dark fens moving
Slow, abstracting
Beneath cold feet,
Their vein-grey streets.

Within the peat
That building heat:
Fire that's never
Extinguished stirs

Giants out of chalk:
Those old neighbours
Baulk at relics
Of fanatics

Long gone – ploughshares
And skirmishes,
Those artefacts:
Roman, Celtic

Embodiment:
None heaven-sent?
Metal and blood
Deny the flood,

And each leaves stains
As the fens drain.
Pipes and ditches
Are their arches:

My formation,
Circulation.
Fleshy flowers
In warm chambers.

Jim Carruth

Because the Land Are We

Because the land
are we:

the days
a gift of breath;

the weeks
muscle burden, sweat;

the months
skin wearing the soil;

the years
hands taking the furrows;

our lifetime
a body harvest-borne;

our death
bones to the earth;

each new voice repeats
the ancient song

*Because the land
are we.*

Mapping
for Bernard

One of the older mothers of the herd
gravity sags your bag below the hocks
calving changes the mammary landscape
so the first milking after you've given birth
becomes a remapping for my hands.

Facing me two standing stones
sturdy back teats now sitting further apart
no longer the pink vertical plumbs
confident way markers for what lies beyond,
for the line of sight has been lost.

I stretch out along the hidden valley
trying to retrace the contours of before
but your wrinkles and veins are a braille
where the language has been changed.

The journey of fingers is an ageing
the haired slopes are not as remembered
for you have entered a new lactation;
how many more cycles are left.

I reach out in memory and grasp nothing
more substantial than an absence
my hand tracks across the hillside
like a shepherd looking for lost sheep
until I brush against one then the other
huddled together as if for warmth.

I welcome them like old friends
I haven't seen all Summer
and wasn't sure were still around
I am happy then to catch up
as they gush forth with stories in milk.

Legacy
for Les M

The banker saw no worth in words
so turned down flat that day
the offer of a farmer's song
as collateral for a loan for seed.

At night the farmer returned home
buried his lyrics across furrows
set never to receive the barley.
By the morning he was gone.

Come the spring in that field
beyond his boarded up house
every small word had sprouted
with such a scent and promise

it brought songbirds flocking
eager to seek each sweet fragment
working the lines day and night
piecing together his old tune.

Until the morning they sang as one
that lost farmer's final crop
for his harvest was their chorus
and they feasted on his song.

Meg Bateman

Touched

I come on crooked-fingered trees,
on lichens and ferns upheld on decay,
each brittle branch in its green muff of moss.
Brown leaf-mould crumbles beneath me
down into gullies, where only the liverwort,
luminous and fleshy, holds on as I slither.
I startle at the sockets in a gleaming skull,
at a heron's harsh cry, try not to let
bog suck and swallow me or root fell me
in the failing light. I clamber over, double
under, sprawling trunks. Brambles
snatch at my sleeves, my hair, in my hurry.
In the undergrowth deer crash. On their trail
I glimpse a hound bounding white, its ears
aglow. The chill air makes me dizzy,
twigs spiral overhead...

It's a relief to see the car through the trees,
get the dog in the back, drop into the seat,
and with radio and heating on,
drive back to concrete and glass,
        hoping colleagues won't notice.

Dilys Rose

Stone the Crows

We really should be more nocturnal. Roosting
at dusk – think what we're missing: mole tartare,
spatchcocked frog, stoat hash! You name it,
somebody's prepped it. The shops are long shut,
the coach parties toddled off. Bobble hat hikers
and twitchers are holed up in B&Bs or the pub.
The night is ours. How's about we break with tradition
and pick up a carryout – fresh kill, still warm?

We make a fetching *Sunset in the Village* shot –
Halloween hunchbacks against a blood orange sky –
but our days in the feathered niche are numbered.
Let's face facts. Us lot won't ever have a say
at a parish council AGM and the mud slingers,
the Johnny-come-lately white settler do-gooders
are set to pass a vote to uproot the trees,
oust us from our nests, asphalt the green.

Before we're homeless, d'you fancy a turn
around the hotspots, tail a couple of 4x4s,
take a butcher's at what's come a cropper –
I can't tempt you? Fair's fair. No need
to be greedy. We've already eaten our fill.
Darlin, I love how you tuck in your wingtips
and snuggle up, but love your hoarse croak more,
your final gripe before darkness undoes us.

Andy Brown

Nocturne

Beyond the ruins of the timber yard
where clumps of rowan, birch and alder
stand ringed with wire against the hungry deer,
the earth is wrought by badger runs.

The dusk is animals – the shrieks of vixens,
owls and fleeting bats – and, if you press
your ear against the evening's broad door
you may hear them: the mother badger,

her heavy skull, her jaws, her glinting teeth
and these, her badger cubs – their mellow baying;
their barrel bodies crashing through the tumps,
writing what they mean in flattened grass.

They grope for teats along her yielding belly,
taking the night on their own terms:
theirs is the world that persists in our absence.
We emerge from the dark with our lamps,

through the gaps in the trees where the copse
meets the meadow and leave them to reclaim
their glade, as dawn grows imperceptibly from night
and presses upwards with the thought of dew.

Pen y Fan

We have been climbing since well before dawn
and now we're alone: the couloir unclouded,
no skirl of wind, and all around a budding
riotousness. Astray in the mountainous heart.

We make the peak and try to fit a landscape
into notebooks. Things emerge out of the blue:
loose ribbons of side-tracks; the glint of gneiss;
a beehive cairn at the precipice edge.

Can anything answer the reason we're here;
the things outside that silhouette the inner?
A cricket chirrs, a raven krekks

caught in the shadow of a simple thought –
wherever we go we are guests to the world
like tufts of sheep's wool snagged on stands of whin.

The Wood for the Trees

Just as what we recognize as *us*
lies outside as much as within,
so those cushions of leaf fall
and humus pile up on the ground

in the forests we've led ourselves into,
where woodpigeons *troo-loo*
and animals and men act out
their uncertain roles. The trees

don't recognize us in any of this:
their polyglot mélange of leaves
describes the light effortlessly.
They have such beautiful handwriting,

the trees. They make their own place
in all this unruliness, forever emerging.
Do we see the trees – the things
themselves – or just a doubtful haze?

The birch trees bend; the wood unlocks.
What we know is a step towards
the prospect of change; putting faith
in the world's offertory box.

Isabel Galleymore

Silvics

We are planted on this earth
the wrong way up:

the tree has it right
though we may not see

its head is in the ground,
limbs cast into the air,

arms and legs sprawling
from its trunk – a sturdy neck

and its mind beneath all this
a taproot at first –

tapering it trickles
a slow burst of thought

which drinks the rich water
held in fracture-cups of rock

or winds around a ruin
swallowed by the soil,

or round a smaller mind, grown
indifferent to her flower dress

her pollen-yellow shoes
gaudy in the sun.

Harvest

After stripping the branches of berries
the robin held a handful of seeds
in its stomach: the robin carried a tree
– in fact she secretly sowed a whole forest –
a store of bows and arrows and shields.
Years found the bird had planted a battle,
its tiny body had borne the new king.

Men looked up to the skies and blessed
or blamed the planets moving overhead.
A blackbird, meanwhile, started to pick
at the fruit both armies had left.

Curculio

Curculio laid her eggs in the core of the nut –
that weightlessly suspended was like a small
planet grown from a hazel tree in the dark. A
hundred ghosts hatched from these tiny eggs:
larvae came crawling from the kernel, the pit,
and grused hungrily through the nut's pale flesh.
They hollowed their way from the inside out,
eventually boring straight through the shell – the
ebonine firmament that wrapped the nut – after
piercing the sky this world of theirs dropped. If
you'd placed a few grubs under a microscope lens
you'd see they had one head with two little eyes,
two arms with hands that crammed their mouths,
two legs on which they walked about.

Jos Smith

Witness

A latter day Noah might have set up camp here,
drunk his wine from a pigskin clenched in a fist,
bitten his lip and drowned that inextinguishable grief.
Here where the Black Ridge slopes to the south
and Hangingstone Hill to the north, a plateau so high
you could see in the fog a god kneel down and deliver
the Okement, the Dart, the Taw, the Teign and the Tavy.

And remember, when the waters were high in the world
the ocean made an island of this moor. And remember,
when the glaciers came down from the north,
dragging their bite across the Earth, they stopped
short of these heights, and shuffled off their moraine.

To these few miles of upland heath, of blanket bog
and valleys draining out toward the sea, is left
the pristine quiet of survival, air with its ears ringing.
As with the prophet whose lot is to live and remember,
an aureole borne so high, pronged with its unscathed
tors, weighs heavy. In such stone, the closed eyes of
gravity; in such stone, silence kept between the teeth.

Ben Smith

from Lessons in Augury

Lesson I: Introductions

Call me Attus Navius. Call me St. Francis of the Birds. Call me Calchas, Tiresias, Laocoon, St. Milburga or Cuthbert of Lindisfarne.

They say I was raised in an eyrie, that I have feathers under my coat. But they soon stop laughing when I see a falcon stoop and send the whole nation to war.

Do you see that kestrel, like a marionette under the clouds? I can show you how to pull the right strings. Give me a pair of hungry rooks and I'll set brother against brother. Father against son. A well trained turtle dove has won me the trust of governors and kings; brought me late-night visits from their daughters and wives. I send my pigeons out at night and they return, heavy with the people's gratitude (in blank envelopes please; in unmarked bills).

Call me Black Elk, Ten Bears, Don Juan Matus. Call me Mopsus, Lizard's Son, Skaay.

I've outlived every one of them and I'm better than them all combined. I can slip outside time like a pocket-watch in a forgotten magpie's nest, like water beading on a cormorant's back.

I've seen other worlds appear in the curve of an iridescent feather. I've watched other pasts and other futures unfold like an albatross' wings. For the right price I can give you vision sharp as a talon, I can teach you how to unwind fate, like wringing a chicken's neck.

Lesson III: Difficult Customers

Everyone likes to think that their fate will be determined by an eagle with a snake in its talons emerging from a blood red sun. Try to temper their expectations. Their future is probably already taking shape, like the crooked mess of a jackdaw's nest in their chimney. Stick by stick. Hour by hour. Like the thump of sparrows flying into closed windows, day after day.

Everyone likes to think that they'd notice it: the briefest of shadows passing over the sun, the flutter of blood suddenly still in the hedges, a single wing-beat – nothing more than a breath – cutting back against the wind. But they just button up their coats or fumble through their pockets, as if searching for something lost. Or find themselves, on starless nights, walking barefoot through fields of corn-stubble, waiting for dark feathers to fall from the sky.

Everyone thinks they can handle the truth; but it can be too much even for us. I knew a great seer who predicted how long he had left. When the day came and nothing happened, he laughed himself to death. I once had a man who couldn't take any more and put a gun to his head. I'd only got as far as explaining the gulls on the fence posts – he never even saw the pheasant on his roof, the line of geese walking in through his half-open door.

I'd like to think you'd be sensitive to the situation. If you foresee happiness and riches, it's best to be sure – book them in for regular readings, arrange a monthly payment plan. But if it all looks bad then I'd tell them straight. Just ask for your fee in advance.

Lesson VIII: Retirement Plans

You'll know when it's time. You'll hear muttering in the palace corridors, like lengths of rope being uncoiled and cut to size. Scaffolding will appear in the temple courtyard and no one will tell you why. You'll hear popping on the phone line. Friends will stop returning your calls. Your letters will arrive days late, crinkled at the edges, re-sealed with glue. When you reach the back door of the minister's offices, someone will have changed the locks.

Don't let them know that you know. Carry on as usual. Make plans for the coming weeks. Even better, let them think that you're losing it. Go out with no socks. Stand all day at the end of your street, mouth open, staring at the sky. Then one night, just leave. Tell no one. Take what you need from your locker at the bus station, your box buried in the allotments. Send anything that you have to the newspapers – stolen files, diaries, taped meetings – this should buy you some time.

Pick a direction and walk. Walk until you reach the mountains. Walk until you reach the sea. Walk until you reach the house that you bought long ago and have kept under a different name. Sleep with your money under your mattress, broken egg shells round your bed. Wake early and watch the road for strangers. Watch the skies. Watch until the gulls flying over are nothing but gulls, the pigeons in the fields nothing but an easy meal.

Wait, like the last time this happened. Over the horizon, cities will rise and fall. Like the tides. Like the leaves falling from the hedges. Like the birds returning, year after year, until one cold bright day they will bring new messages, like voices suddenly clear over the radio after a long night lost in static.

Terry Jones

Economies

This autumn economy whispers to itself,
secrets of gold, lost liquidities,
vexed branches visible in cold sunlight
and nests stood naked to the wind. Is it true still
the single value of a leaf is spent where it lands?
I bring in Raymond Glasson, old dyker,

fence-builder, countryman of Burnrigg:
once, when he needed the pay,
he pushed his hand in the hedge to be cut,
found it curled it round a sparrow's nest;
its warmth in his palm like the tit of his first girl,
he left it there in its quiet, went unpaid.

I saw him down at his allotment this evening,
the year's graph falling about him where he worked
close to home. This is time for mulch protection,
graftings, new plantings, dormant perennials:
– those and a nest left alone.

Five eggs, I think he said, speckled and tiny.

Awkward Bird

The seasons are not compelled to run sideways
Wind double back on itself
Crops turn to yellow in the fields
And the river change its mind
There is nothing flying but the awkward bird of ourselves

The trees and their leaves have no whimsy
Mad in the Winter – Yes
In Spring singing molten flowers
And all their straining chorus
There is nothing flying but the awkward bird of ourselves

The bronze leaf of the chestnut is spinning
bluebells stand in world-heavy dark
Above all there are shadows and more
There is nothing flying but the awkward bird of ourselves

Bee

i

It's a matter of where you tread
nothing is hurt
nothing touched if you missed the nest
hid under the iron hearts of flowers
scaffold eyes on a root
and until you heard it
your ear would be in the dark
a bee coming in
on an unsettlable drone
for its version of the sweet

ii

one I locked in a bottle
settled and lifted
its furious resonance held
on the draught of itself
where it hung then hit and hit
the inconceivable
atheist on an invisible wing
without dying a bee
will save its sting
for the real

iii

Is it saying 'am' or 'om'
after its dance zooming
east or west?
hands curled in yellow-black fur
you could ride a bee
to the holy doorway of its hive
hold the note and enter

Chris McCully

Watching White-trout on the River Dargle
for Éamon de Buitléar

Their lives were made before they lived them.
While Troy torched laughter onto a girl's cheeks;
throughout the centuries-long scourging of the Christ;
when Tara was erected from the Arctic river
and became the government of Orion –
restless, unwitting, they were doing the same,
their shadows nuzzling gravel under the alder.

For new gods and dispensations they care nothing.
There's only the gap where they're nagged
by gravity, whose tides fetch sandeels
from the anemone's maw; where the flea
leaks at last into rotting plankton.
That's where they have to go, into the galleries
of extinction, the guddling of Odin's eye.

And now they lie in three yards of water
whose surface the clouds preen. Even at rest
they're all nerve. One wrenches its belly on the stones
to rub at lice – a fetish where the moon grimaces.
So kyped his jaws won't close, another grins
at what was wrought before the gods were gods,
when white-trout were flaws in molten glass:

the inscription of hunger, the sour flood,
archaeology of the redd, starlight
churning in the guts whose compulsions
were unanswerable and became his shoal.
At last he's hulled with his useless weapons.
What keeps him alive is what will kill him:
winters; spawning; reaching home.

Gerry Loose

from Fault Line

XLVII

at the head of the glen
just east of the reservoir dam
at a spur of a track
west of powerlines
defining ministry land
246935 written
below a triangle
on a scrap of paper
during manoeuvres
Maol Odhar
an unfulfilled prophecy
file & rasp of duck song
click & rattle of magpie
sweet in the ear of the glen

commentary:

what are the articles (& of war)
falcons on thermals of hot breath
not reasoned but felt
not felt but experienced
not experienced lived
not lived endured

XLVIII

among fleabane
among vetch
among deceivers
at the heart of it

commentary:

a ring of smoke
a wren's broken eggshell
sea mammal vertebra
fail-chuach
a scented bowl
place enough

XLIX

welcome guests
caterpillar on the dinner kale
snail on a freshly felled tree bole
fires for winter
after next
liberated

commentary:

in blackness
of a black round moon
there below trees
in head redness throbbing
swans lay their eggs

LI

sea mist
lifting a little
black with cancer
a prisoner
goes home to die
the President
declares compassion
to be a mistake

commentary:

heterophonic
once culture here
psalm 79 sung
unaccompanied
men much given to whisky
crackling in mouths
of farmers the gaelic
chewing thistledown
spitting warheads
none to bury them

LXVIII

how clear shadow is
clearer than lined hand
than veined leaf
than handbones
held to shade eyes

commentary:

stolen expressions
of existence
there's one whose name is lost
Tharsuinn the crosswise hill
& Auchengaich
Chaorach hill of the fank
Maol an Fheidh bleak hill of the deer
the dappled hill
Creag Madaidh little crag of the fox
& the lookout hill of the sheiling
here's the stony hill
the high cracked hill
the red hill & the black hill crowding
litter of the shoreline
Coulport
& Faslane the homestead of sorrows

LXIX

many dogs travel
on the ferry
with passengers
eating breakfast
watching clouds
mushroom

commentary:

sudden oak death
& they're on edge
round the corner
deep horizon
never to apprehend
the abundant numinous
now

LXX

kyriekyrie
in greenblue confusion
a kingfisher
singing a pitched song
sounding like anger
to those out of tune
compressed signals
the frequency of
windscream in halyards

commentary:

to act is &
to dream
what is said
by the invisible

LXXI

the Minister calls
for a lesser capacity
to kill 38 million people
not the full 51 million
the President smiles

commentary:

paper not stone
skin not paper
brain *and* skin
who'd stop the
leaves swarming
he asked

LXXII

a lute
hanging in a wind
bent blackthorn
on autumn
fugitive hills
gods & heroes
like any other refugees
the President smiles
solvet saeculum in favilla

commentary:

gu'n airigh
at the high
summer pastures
wood sorrel
for children
transhumance
cup & ring marks
bullet pocks

LXXIII

gulls follow the plough
that guns be used
only for the firing of seeds
willowherb down
as if for
borrowed time
the day's work
6 coach screws
sent home into
roof trusses
free//for less
than a clock's single tock
ashes postponed

commentary:

going backwards
dances of hills
movements
& the verb
of the cold hill
the bald hill

LXXIV

this lyre
this lute bothers me
not even sweet
as a swan hooting
through her nostrils
feet slapping water in
the effort to fly
to sing to rise

commentary:

suddenly
since it's all not there
there's nothing
no harebell
no hill
as sudden
there's hill
there's summer
furze
no thing
unadorned unborn
mind
but caring what happens
as if for love
practising
as if for compassion
don't be scared
as if for a single
raindrop
out in the firth

Susan Rowland

For the Forest

The creek is my thin glass arm
Where I eat stones.
My breath calcifies
Into white oak,
Wrinkled, serpentine,
Aged with moss and fern,
Its twisted sinews
A mouth for clouds.
My belly heaves
And the black earth splits open,
Exposing root muscles,
Deep hot rocks, blood
And seeds warm as eggs.
The sun and moon are my breasts,
Their juices infuse the trees,
Thicken into pearls, dabs
Of light that flame
The spirits of the forest.
I know my bones are made
Of mountains still stuck
With snow.
I found my navel in a crater
Of blue rain,
Every night my waters lick the stars
From the sky's skin.

What the Trees Want

We know the trees can create new creatures
From us, just as their blood spatters
When the axe bites and they become bone.
On wooden gallows, we are the hanged man,
Dead trunk, empty
By penetration of tree flesh.
Trees want us to be wild, to know roots
That nourish the underworld and feed on
Deep waters, pure and freezing, out of rock.
Trees are baskets for the sun, their leaves
Sift and winnow light, alchemical colours feather
The forest shadows.
Trees summon the moon into the sky
And blow the seeds of radiance
Into that sad soil: Lady Moon dances for them.
The oldest trees can talk to stars,
Their cracked bark bears the scars
Of human history,
They are trying to forgive us.

Run Your Hands...

Run your hands in my sweet sap
As we entwine strong roots,
Snakes that eat stars
And unwrap the sky
To commingle continents.
Your damp forest has mossy columns;
It builds halls in my dry woods,
Stabs green life into old earth.
My white skin flowers in your arms,
I hold you like a river,
Sowing rain in a great drought.
Entangled, we rock like the sea,
Have tamed a storm,
Our lips burn together.

Sharon Black

Dharma

These mountains are Buddhas, recumbent
on tatamis of woven rush
laid out across the temple of this valley
under a hand-painted ceiling of blue.

Our home, a fold in this one's robe;
that cloud, a handkerchief drifted from his pocket;
even the bees drone to a slumber
as they waft in on his breath.

His brow is smooth as a prayer flag,
his belly shimmers in the heat.
He is dreaming cicada and birdsong.

Fingal's Cave

Staffa is the grinning mouth
of a whale. Our boat edges in
through a knocked tooth, on a tongue of sea
– we admire its glottis, its palate,
its idle breath.

And later as we sit Jonah-like
on basalt dentistry,
our heads raised towards a guano fresco
on the ceiling, we hear it:

an echo of Mendelssohn,
the drone of a church organ
as if the island were calling us to prayer.

Charles Wilkinson

from THE MARCHES

SONNET III – 'AND SHE REACHED DOWN FROM THE LADDER TO HOLD.'

Reversed Elizabethan

    wafers of **lost** garden leaves that line
    orchards once em**bossed** with the golden
yes apples flashed with the light **teem**ing
through clouds that went to sea o hundreds
of years ago: **seam** of soft earth un-
dulation: forgotten winds **blew** through
grasses **hair** branches touched his hand reach-
ing for was it gleam **fruit** alchemy
on the bough or hand playing **air**
with tender fingers? yet love's **loot** un-
stringed is stolen all again all gone
to need **now** in the cellar cobwebs
cling to wines that age so far above
the ladder in *land that's lost to **plough**.*

STRATA: SONNET III RE-VERSED

beneath the house loves lies in strata

    once gardens orchards wood's lit bluebells
flame of wild flower sun-flooded leaf
& unwinking objects lost in shade
    for the light mislaid its searching eye

this intaglio lost its Roman
    the ring slips over a knuckle-stone
silverhead's sealed with his kingdom
    lawns and lovers time-turned weather vane

forest so deep in silence fields red soil
    year the oak sailed with the Armada
the wooden ladder leant against a tree
    her hand plucked evening-sun apple

orchard playing blossom & strings of light
    his arms stretched tenderly to catch her
did she step down, scorning upturned palms
    blue shadows of leaves faced either way

or do their once sweet thoughts rise through earth
    the broken rungs are all *changed to coal*
yet raise a glass and so to repose
    rooms rest still, now charged with happiness

love lies in strata beneath the house

The Happiness Over the Hill

    a sun the colour of a fox shows
how light is darker than we think, slink-
    ing day towards night; yet the snow on
the mountains is as white as these pills,
    a circle of small planets, resting
on the palm, a promise of balance;
    just when the shadows stretch like water,
there's something spreading: this used to be
    called happiness, see it leavening
on the top of the cloud; though the gold
    evening leaking will service, here's
something darker in the mix: there is
    rain, chemical in the sunlight that
falls, fixing rainbows in hidden fields.

Ariel Gordon

SEMIOVIPAROUS
For my daughter, sleeping in the car.

O Anna. In late spring, ponds are full
of broken broom-handles
& sodden wrapping-paper tubes & none of us
believe in lurid shoots or rootstalk's
floury sustenance or even babies
that get up hours after birth.
But out in the pasture, afterbirth cures
like sausage between the bison's legs
as her kinked calf hobbles over ruts
& wallows. Footsore, bored,
you spin so you can fall
& you spin so you can see me again & again
& you spin to spin & fall, laurelled
with sere grasses
& attention.

When the calf is eight months old
its headbutts to its dam's udder
will almost unseat her
the bison will be almost as bruised
as when she presented herself to the prairie
backside open & raw.

In late spring, ponds fill
with lusty frog-song & shorebirds shriek
sleek counterpoint at flashes of leg
at the eyeless lids of opening leaves
& the sound washes over me
as though through skin.

The pond offers marbled sheets of algae
& water weed, silence & din
& I want to stay. Your dad carries you away
but you believe in me even through a screen of willow,
its branches buckshot with galls:
Mum-mum! Mum-mum!

Out in the pasture, the bison is delivered
from the sway of her pregnant sisters
& stands apart. *Mum-mum!* The calf,
sensitive to haunch & hip,
to fillips of movement
jumps as the tractor works the other half
of their range, as I give up,
O Anna & cart you off.

How to Survive in the Woods

Tip #2: Stand still and look around carefully! Wherever you are will become your 'point zero.' Find a way to mark it using a spare piece of clothing, a pile of rocks, a sheet of paper, or anything else easily visible from a distance.
                    wikiHow, How to Survive in the Woods.

In the woods, the man who yanked off
his pants to spook fat dog walkers
& ancient slow birders
can't get it up. Nearby, the foreleg of a deer in a tree,
the first joint cleaned to the bone.

The furred knee hung over a knot
is a drunk uncle leaning close to say, *Nice gams!*
Knowing the poacher is stiff
with satisfaction at the gesture. And the woods are lousy
with teenagers, fingering guns of compressed air
& held breaths, so the first time
the woods come out & ask *Who are you?*
its green voice breaks.

You can marshal yourself against the bloody leer
of unleashed dogs, the gnashed throats
of mallards, but you can't plan for the glimpse
between trees
of childhood in the clearing,
the slide of city shoes on the shield's chipped teeth,
how the word *wild* has begun to beg, as a half-starved
bear begs: defeated, but with one eye
on the toddlers & lap dogs.

How to Water Your Lawn Effectively

1. Drink so much water that you run clear & mark your territory, you dribbling homeowner you.

2. Being neither a cooper nor a carpenter, invest in (the sour emptiness of) whiskey barrels. Invest in eaves, mulch plugs, ladders with slippery rungs – no ladder! – the intersect of lightning & elm canopy.

3. Your neighbour's hose, 4am. (Dreams of running water, of loss.)

Mouth to bronze spout, you know: this is what happens when the nail in your veins is loosened.

This is the taste of a mouthful of change.

4. Rip out grass like carpet, like end-roll hastily bought & rejected by the next tenant who 'has an eye for these things.' Tramp dirt, raising peaty clouds & lining your mouth with sod.

5. Avoid relationships with classical scholars prone to grand gestures or at least get one on a low-sodium diet.

6. Ask a farmer if you can pick rocks (his fields overturned, rocks come to the surface as teeth come through gums).

Don't think about drunks, vitrines & convenient projectiles.

Later, train moss onto your rocks the way you train pets onto paper.

7. Lie on the lawn, aching & chill. Turn on the sprinkler.

When your hair is plastered among blades broad & wet, your fingers twined with half-drowned worms, turn off the damn water.

David Troupes

from GOD OF CORN

Each of these poems begins with a passage from Josiah Gilbert Holland's 1865 multi-volume book A History of Western Massachusetts.

MOUNT POMEROY AND MOUNT LIZA

Mount Pomeroy and Mount Liza lift their peculiar conical forms, about a mile and a half apart, each holding company with the tradition that gave it its name. Mount Pomeroy received its name, it is said, from a combat which a man of that name had with a bear upon its territory, and Mount Liza perpetuates a part of the name of Elizabeth, the name of an Indian captive who was buried there.

Gun in hand out the door and the raw
grows worse. The lessening
of November, the strick of wind
crowding and dividing the reeds. The town
passes quickly.
Into the woods now, where the trees are keys
all fitted to locks.
In a damp saddle between hills, among the hemlocks
are turkeys. Therefore the gun. Therefore
hope,
and the wincingness of sound.
Spent candles line the fir-sills.
We settle, a carcass
in repose, patient among the seeps
for our chance. We find mothers

in strange places,
and they raise strange sons. Rain
darkens the wood and glitters the fern.
Silence from the root-hovels.
The man who fought, the girl who died
are not a mind of light touching
hill to hill, are not
a weed flagging in the wet.
They are nowhere, are nothing.
Softly,
silently across the needles
turkeys roll their barrels of blood.
Our muscles tighten to our bones.
There is your mountain, son.
So climb.

This Quarry Is Not

This quarry is not at present worked to its fullest capacity, but when the demand for the stone shall require it, the marble can be quarried almost to an indefinite extent.

Gently
almost we
take the world apart,
as though one day to turn it all around
and put everything back together.
A fluted column,
a plinth for glory. Dust
is a problem and the men
wrap rags around their mouth and foreheads
like ramshackle crowns. Their faces
and eyes

are red, a punched-about look,
a rawness of sun.
There is a tent over the water barrels
and ladles and cloths, and spilled water runs
from the shade
to the heat
where the air takes it, or it settles away
among the gravel. My mother
died in a glory of home,
in a frame of rafters and ribs. But what got me, really
what killed me
almost was my father's stopped face—
the unfussy surrender
of the old man at his window with his sky.

THE LAND DESIGNATED IN THE DEED

The land designated in the deed as Quana *is the middle meadow, adjoining Agawam meadow.* Usquaiok *is Mill River and the lands adjoining it.* Nayasset *is 'the three corner meadow and land adjoining, extending Northerly to Chicopee River.'* Massaksicke *is the 'long meadow', and now bears the latter name as a town.*

The river rests upon the meadow a few days in a year.
Evening of evening.
Nothing has been buried here, nothing at all
and not once. Grasses
ebb and eel. The sun
is weakened by March, healed by March,
throwing light
little more than shadow, and the reeds
stand like men bearing witness. Dying is only
living and nothing
has been buried here, nothing laid down, nothing

set aside.
Weeds in a frail cotillion.
Millwork of sky.
The sun has made a promise to the river's dark
box of ribbons, its beads
and threads. The root has made a promise
to the tongue. So
does the shaken hand shake the meadow,
a nervous breeze. So
does the signed paper join
the other husks and flags. So through us
does the river weep of itself, betrayed,
a grief of current.
The meadow swallows back its love and its hate.
Leaves toll their traffic of sugar.
The shot crow
sprawls in the rut, jewelled with ants, an image
of herself alive.

Arpine Konyalian Grenier

IF NOT, WINTER

The world could have been a ball floating over water
could have towered Americanly about truth & logic
what comes to mind naturally obstacle I posit
a social versus natural phenomenon
Ecclesiastes breathes

                        defined by it

the industrial production numbers are in
floating desire on top some melody
to recognize and hence distance
to ground the intended
memorial

countrymen beholden to townspeople
around food climate occupation
neither mourning nor refusing
the possibility of knowing
the cautionary

        peel away possibility

no greater effort requires solidarity then
regard less the ice cap's meltdown
truth comes to mind naturally
the fall defining we exist
just because

as love is to heart authority is to a state
living the tribal social
we must build over

bare necessity
one cannot hoard as it does not predicate
states or statements
the Adamly

        transcribed in charity
            pauses

pare pare down

                dead leaf

        butterfly

  paper

        kite butterfly

        when is a qualifier excluded
December to January American Tropical Blue.

Hit by Her Ancient Wings

Dissertation lily in hand I remain biblical as I am not
the me that feeds on the rest of me
the provisional setup meanwhile
blighted chance I settle for
the lesser a sin to be
cloud extruded

    average state in accord

the one that maintains the rests of me having lived
my only need is adjunct and *ad valorem* it says
carefully waking but not getting up
(what are you going to do without
cognition under the pillow?)

use it as means not end
    I admonish the clock that reminds

as Hu I float quantum ready what inevitable erg
post Hu declares for action and other minds
and if I pull being away what then?

        the sinuating

your many faces unable to die for
acts of recognition

    faintly exchanges
                redress

drag an imaginary sun void of course and keel
navigate/ negotiate the otherwise muscular
four lettered for uncut bone
light repeating need

    disallows

self scribed and non-directional
anterior to the experience

    I confess to some heart

there is no intelligence in being I declare
my brain & eyes softwared for solution
intelligibility startles and scares
begging and yes ignorant
illusion is hardware

here and there cocoons in tempered states
mourn the experience written off or by
a because for lack of criminality
judge me on that object

participant of mediocrity that I am
anticipant of excellence that I
sanction without naming

                incessantly

my safety my debit card as selfish act
software has rendered corrupt
off course and over

sine waves notwithstanding
every inch the proverbial

servile comes to mind
curves a surprise

                found emotion

a dying act hovering
larger and larger
tracking.

Flatly Present my Shame

I am afraid of the hill I am
of the city on the hill

a marker of heaven and earth

community based vigilance and thought
abridged for presence and complexity

please save me please I'm served
a conquer or perish dish daily

shapes flatten unto a screen
connectivity breeds collapse
patterns vie for content
profiles everywhere

how can one abridge a pixel?
who do they belong to?

do you want a place in history?

breed consumption earth cannot afford
presence patterned after self as object
come consume combat collapse
else as tagged convenient
unique and interior

permit me to save lives

the rest of our footage rests on it
light around light musculateral
wall reaching for

as domestic as organic a place

as place a veil is lifted and lost
away from corpuscular legality
place as lack thereabouts
lost to demons error
error what makes
a great wall

metonymy
tin pan lyrics

flesh endures but cannot hold
homo hetero auto the sound
give me a second look
son et lumiere.

Howard Giskin

Mountain Lion Tracks

The animal was nowhere in sight
though could have been there moments

before or hours past; tracks
were fresh for snow had fallen

I stopped and stared silently
into the distance at the hills and

houses; air crisp smoke from
chimneys hovering in the morning

curiously I recall nothing
of the rest of the walk; when I

think of this place joy invades my mind.

Pine Barrens

Gliding down river past
lush green sandy banks
river courses rust
colored over smooth
pebbles at night whippoorwills
crying darkness stars moon
over paths swimming
naked you and I
cruising pines in a
flatbed truck in cool
night air green dark immersed
enveloped flowing
memory can't see bottom
cloaked ring of sand scent
of earth smoke water and quiet
mud and the crackle of fire.

Rupert M Loydell

Bright Currency
(Gunwalloe)

Slate books libraried in the sand:
easy-to-collect smooth circles of stone.
The sea writes them as it rolls towards the shore.

It's harder to find triangles,
uncomfortable three-edged pebbles
resistant to curves.

Beach almost to myself,
I own the bright currency of poverty,
debts all washed away.

Apples, Storm, Adventure

Apples turn to cider
on the mossy path
in the abandoned orchard.

I didn't know where to go
as the path meandered
through broken glass
then past the empty beehive.

No warning lights;
the shining stranger
sings in lightning and in rain.

There is never enough thunder
and always too much noise,
some kind of sound sculpture
half-built on the muddy lawn.

Once we all agree
then this rain will stop
and the slow blues begin.

I wish I could decide
which branches the fruit would fall from,
choose the spot where it would land
but as we all know by now,

time and change is an adventure
echoing in another's mind. I love you
but don't know what to say.

Alec Finlay

WIND-SONGS

i

I say *can you hear the wind?*
she says *it's the wind*

ii

the gust's disturbed motion
is an invisible influence
that would pass unknown

but for the shush of strewn leaves
and whine of wires
that the night mixes

with the turbine's wavering hum
and the juddering rattle
of its pinched blades

while this wind still blows
we know there will be
no end to change

iii

with time
& economies
of scale
sweeping sails

of cloth
were refined
to falling
blades of steel

iv

even wind's stochastic complexity
can be reduced to a continuum
of needle & spindle

out on the hills and moors
windmill rotors sweep
their tips against the orison

modulating a measure of weather
on the climactic fringe
of the carbon era

v

the far sky stretches amplitudes
of cloud over Aegean atolls
marked by wind-towers

Rousay, Westray
Papa Westray
Stronsay, Eday

keeping hold of the big idea
someday each isle will be under sail
with a tower of its own

the three blades of each island
turbine turning, ushering in
another triquetra era

vi

wind prevailed and, in time,
so did knowledge, manifest
in the azure prospect of Burgar Hill

where turbines wheel
their arms over and again
like big kids in the sun

from the brow of Costa Head
facts and figures were exchanged
with pioneers around the globe

their successes and failures
demonstrating how time and motion
could contain a sustaining logic

their culculations a foundation
that set wind-towers revolving
and produced the profusion of designs

of the domestic turbines that tirl
in the mirr of the outset isles
in today's winds & tomorrow's gales

Notes: *Burgar Hill, Orkney, pioneering wind turbine test-site of the 1980s; Costa Head, Orkney, experimental test-station, site of Britain's first windmill turbine, c. 1950, established by E. W. Golding O.B.E. (c. 1900–1965), director of the British Electrical and Allied Industries Research Association.*

John Glenday

Only a leaf for a sail, and before us,
look, the impossible ocean of it all;
squall and storm; lash and flail; the
unnavigable, the hungry, the whole
perfect unstarred bleakness of the
world, as though a dark we feared had
been made real and cold and tidal, and
the lifted green black ragged face of
its hand to pull us, pull us down, and
what chance would you say we had, so
small, only the two, my love. Just me.
Just you. But give us a leaf for a sail,
and suddenly, somehow, everywhere's
possible.

Allt Dearg

This burn runs dark
and sweet as the lining
of the soul.

Drink from me
And you will always
be thirsty.

Birch Wind

Just a touch of air in the birch trees
lets them sing their ragged moment;
catches the trim of the early leaves,
passes on; likewise all the stuff of
me is stirred, lit and purposed, all
my being someone, grown. This
breath of air through the reed of a
tapered leaf, is a shred of song half
sung towards everything but itself;
always almost heard and almost
always gone.

Jorie Graham

Of Inner Experience

Eyes shut I sense I am awakening & then I am
        awake but
        deciding
to keep eyes shut, look at the inside, stay inside, in the long and dark of it,
        if it were a garden what would I plant
        in it, for now I am
alive I think I feel who among you will tell me
        after all this time
the difference & yet again now I am alive & what does that mean lying here eyes
        closed first winter morning coming on all round,
        yes, this is the start of winter is what
        my body
        sensing a new dis-
equilibrium says, hypnotized, trembling with fiction, love, the sensation of time passing,

                              & fear of a-
                              temporality, *& this is*
                              the play of heaven the mind in-
                              side this body lying here still
                              alive for
                              now

thinks—if you could only see my body and beyond me the three windows in the room
                              letting the uninvented
                              in—and how true *it* is
                              because of the closed

eyes on my human being lying there in the room glistening with plenitude, all conquest
gone from the air—you could say here god owns everything, it is a discharge of duration,
                      the floor the panes the mirror the single stalk of
freesia the gilded frame the two lionclaw-footed chairs and the tree-knots
                            still in
                        the floors someone laid in 1890, the

wormholes here and there in them from those creatures' work long ago, not long after the
counter-revolution, the troubles—& the wreck here of consciousness—as long as the
                              person's eyes

stay shut—beyond the limits of thought—(& who am I
then?)(& don't go there says my hand as I need it, my
hand, here in this
writing)—and yet

I am also lying on the bed eyes closed
and keeping them so, god owes us
everything I
think from out here, there is not god I think lying in the non-dark of the mind, eyes
closed, hearing the crows rustling in
the nearest
trees, the hayfork in the next field—I want to pray says the person behind the eyes—you

cannot do so I say with these fingers—I want to break the dark with the idea of God says the

non-sleeping person on her back in the beginning of the 21st century, trying to hold onto

duration which is slipping, slipping, as she speaks as I write, active translator, look
I can make a tale of the sinking sun I can begin
summer again here are its
swallows they have

      just returned
      look
up—but no, they did not come back after that one year, we waited—but here they
        are again, do not be
        fooled, and breaking their circles
across the evening air, and there is still sun up near the children's bedtime, we still say
        bedtime, it is a habit, and the bells
ring vespers, or the recording of it, and somewhere there must still be a crafty
        animal digging a long tunnel under
this strange hard ground, finding some moisture in there, turning it, grain by grain,
          perhaps there is still
          the creature
          which when it
          was known
          was known as
          the blind mole
          somewhere.

The Bird That Begins It

In the world-famous night which is already flinging away bits of dark but not
        quite yet
        there opens
        a sound like a
        rattle, then a slicing in which even the
        blade is

audible, and then again, even though trailing the night-melt, suddenly, again, the
        rattle. In the

night of the return of day, of next-on time, of
        shape name field
        with history flapping
        all over it

invisible flags or wings or winds—(*victory* being exactly
        what it says,
        the end of night),

(it is not right to enter time it mutters as its tatters

                    come loose)—in the
                    return I
                    think *I
                    am in this body*—

I really only think it—this body lying here is
                    only my thought,
                    the flat solution
                    to the sensation/question
                    of

who is it that is listening, and who is it that is wanting still
                    to speak to you
                    out of the vast network
                    of blooded things,

a huge breath-held, candle-lit, whistling, planet-wide, still blood-flowing, howling-silent, sentence-driven, last-bridge-pulled-up-behind city of
                    the human, the expense-
                    column of place in
                    place humming…To have
                    a body. A borderline

of ethics and reason. Here comes the first light in leaf-shaped coins.
They are still being flung at our feet. We could be Judas no
                      problem. Could be
                      the wishing-well. Right
                      here in my open
mouth. The light can toss its wish right down this spinal
                      cord,
                      can tumble in
and buy a wakened self… What is the job today my being
                      asks of
                      light. Please
tell me my job. It cannot be this headless incessant crossing
                      of threshold, it cannot be
                      more purchasing of more
good, it cannot be more sleeplessness—the necklaces of
                      minutes being tossed
                      over and over my
                      shoulders. The snake

goes further into the grass as

                                    first light hits.
                                    The clay
in the soil gleams where dew withdraws. Something we don't want
                                                      any more of
                                                      flourishes as never
                                                      before. I
                                                      feel the gravity
                                                      as I sit up
                                                                         crackles on the sill. Preparation
like a leaf growing from the stalk of the unknown
still lying there behind me where sleep just was. Daylight
                                                                             of day
                                                                             everywhere
                                                                             underfoot. Across
the sill, the hero unfolding in the new light, the
                                                                         girl who would
                                                                         not bear the
                                                                         god a

son, the mother who ate her own grown

                    flesh, the god
                    who in exchange
for Time gave as many of his children as need be
                            to the
                            abyss. It is
                            day.

The human does not fit in it.

Earth

Into the clearing shimmering which is my owned
                lawn between
                  two patches of
                    woods near

dawn clock running as usual the human in me
                watching as usual
                for

everything to separate from everything again as light
                comes back
                and the dark

which smothers so beautifully the earth lifts and all is put
                on its leash
                again one
                long leash

such as this sentence—and
                into the open beyond my window-

        pane the new
        day comes as if
        someone its constant
        master
calls—it never refuses, lingers, slows, it doesn't
        abandon us—and I see it, the planet, turn
        through the barely lifting latex
        shade, and the just-rising sunbeam-sliver like a
        nail-trim move
across the tree-grain on the floor across those hundreds of
        years of molecules
        sucking-in water and light—
        this slightly
C-shaped edge of the billion-light-year-toss-of-a-coin—
        sometimes trembling a
        bit if the shade
        lets in wind—
        inexorably—
and I see you my planet, I see your exact rotation now on my

floor—I will not close these eyes in this my
head lain
down on its
sheet, no, its

sleeplessness will watch, under room-tone,
and electromagnetism,
the calculations fly off your flanks as you
make your swerve,
dragging the increasingly

yellow arc across the room here
on this hill and
I shall say now

because of human imagination:
here on this floor this
passage is
your wing, is
an infinitesimal
strand of a feather in
your wing,

this brightening which does not so much move, as
    the minute hand
    near my eye
    does, as it
glides—a pulling as much as a pushing—of event—
    so that you are never
    where you just were and yet
    my eye has not
moved, not truly, is staying upon your back and riding you—
I don't want the moon and the stars, I want to lie here arms
    spread
    on your almost eternal
    turn
and on the matter the turn takes-on as it is turned by that
    matter—Earth—as
    my mind lags yet
    is always
on you, and the lag is part of the turn, its gold lip
    less than an

arm's length from me
now so that I
can dip my fingers right out
into it
as we
orbit the
oval hoop and

the silence in here is staggering—

how huge you
carrying

me are—and there is

never hurry—
and nothing will posit
you as

you carry the positors—as you carry the bottom
of the river and its
top and the clouds
on its top, watery, weak, and the clouds one looks up to
to see

                    as they too

                    turn—

and you are not hunted—not hunting—not

                    hungry—

                    and you want

                    no

thing—are almost mute—(this is to be

                    considered)—

                    and the churchbells in

                    this of your

time zones (to praise what

                    exactly) begin

                    and to

                    one place heavy

                    rains are

                    coming now,

                    and a horse

is riding wildly through one of your

                    darknesses,

                    its horseman praying fiercely
                    to get there
                    in time,
                    to that some-
                    where
else which is you, still you, only you,
                    in which only he
                    could be
                    for all eternity
                    too late.

Gordon McInnes

Held and Held in Place
Coatham Dunes & The German Charlies

      cormorants bob amongst the iron-slag
         dumped into the sea
            scuttled ores spent of metal
              coastal defence turned mussel beds
              awash with the sediments of dredging
             buttress for the fragile dunes
            that ridge inland
            defilades of knitting shoots
            strand line vegetation
            patchwork spots of lyme link marram
           sea sandwort, marsh orchid, oraches
          the first colonisers
         clustered scrub
        huddling into wind-breaks
      digging down to be
     held and held in place
    resistance accumulating
establishing new roots

Slem

Definition: Mud-flat; Unreliable, Untrustworthy.

a man
furtive on the track

a bag
flung out from the bank –

slack mire
boat sputter

too bare to be called
fen

testing depth
step by step

merging into parts
sucking
oozing
dense

wader
sediment

legs
smothered under
a water-puckered
press

sluiced into the lashed
mud-flat
made
un-made
brackish
broken
tracked

    a swithering of elements
    bare and river fed:

    slem

    and looking in the bag?

    one kitten still alive
    five dead.

Mark Goodwin

Pity & Wild

*We are fallen in mostly broken places, but the wild
can still return us to ourselves.*
                                            Robert Macfarlane

      step from a house   pass

through a rim
of a town   follow

a long on
going river   now

            alone imagine

out of sight
& earshot

                 among a vast

far off marsh
wind pulls

      tears from a you   smears

your cheeks   pretend
to cry for creatures

now some un
fathomable wild fixes

                your gaze or

     what a you thinks
     a you sees

a heron's mistaking some
version of *you* for a fish

eyeballing a you
through your eye

                      and there's pity

pity wriggling silver
but only in some

      human's tear

now some you weeps   really
sobs like some child

            for billions of creatures

     some you feels

your bones & all
bones as be

                   longing like stone

pity hits you
pity's face

           familiar

as your mother's or
some mother of

                          some you

and now a you knows
it   a you

      only pities

                       creatures called people   a

you breathes   a
you breathes just

       like a hunted hare

listen!

      that

      gasp   a gasp

      called yours

                    only the wild in a world is safe

         wild *will*

         take all
         who are

         & that is
         yours

Mario Petrucci

two poems for a newborn son

close in   in

pungent waves you
enter   as i lean
to breathe

you breath
-perfumed your
aromas skimmed kin

-like from that benthic
bulk you are to
molecules

sealing their
salts beneath skinned
light or squirming shoals

corpuscular under salten
burdens your lymph
circulates as

turtle or salmon
cogent in whatever
underwatered bodies must

do you drowse as aware
as the egg that sleeps
inside the egg :

your pink-lit
   face reduced &
   reflected zeroed

   in this eye

when milk enters

blood as floes that
blob lesser &
rounder into

reddened sea
so your far-shrilled
gull motions in circles to

whittle stillness then
drop to a pose
abruptly

local
quelled one
legged at an edge to

glance down-up this
main-street melt
whose vast

white Moores
loom & glob glide
purposefully south as

slugs diminish through
light salt-porous as if
waiting were due

till one suck
-sigh from waves
north-keeping rheums

the child-lucent span to
temperate foam
fizzes

to deep
water your fast
-shrinking ice-aspirin

of unsleep

Ian Seed

Senza Risposta

Reshaping the way, or merely a bridge
to a tree which seems to be leaning
sodden at the edge of a small crowd?

We can already name its story, though
we can't yet read its tiny print. But how
to describe the bones of the children

who once called to each other in a forest
where now steel bodies move along
through threads of rain? Such absences

make us. From this spot here we are there
at the bridge, touching. But are we freer
than the leaves that float below? The bridge,

if true, will let the stream run its course.
Invisible children will brush by, wander
on to redraft the real world.

Allen Tullos

Data Points Cloud the Event Horizon

Every thread of summer is at last unwoven.
           Wallace Stevens

What's it raining about?
When to tap Dumb Luck's shoulder?
Pundits at the Whether Channel
on spiral staircases of melanogaster,
toss around the urge to be ancestorless.
Death is one thing,
an end to birth is something else.

Some foreclosed forest root rot,
packing its unread virtue,
a might-could-have-been
from miniscule swirled
(benefit, unlike risk
is not a term of probability),
gives up its sedentary kernal
to roving bands of cumulatives
jockeying fast-moving fronts.

The wind that shakes the particulates.
The squirrel's heartbeat.
Every code of life at last broken,
flabergastrologists ready realignments.
There is currently no tutorial
on how to activate system restore.

Cathleen Allyn Conway

The Pageant

We nineteen are feted to a luncheon in the library
where they conduct the private interviews, asking
why we want to be this year's 'Diana of the Dunes'.

We are not asked which berries are edible, what fish
Michigan stocks, or how to survive with less than
a blanket, a jelly glass, a knife and two guns.

So no one answers how oaks turn crimson and maples gold,
how the sand eats the beach grass, the trees, the road;
they don't know of Alice Gray – or of her unmarked grave.

Backstage we are painted in Mary Kay samples, a procession
of old bridesmaid dresses and last year's prom gowns.
The crowned 'Diana' will cut ribbons, wave from parade floats,

while the ghost of Diana streaks from her driftwood
cottage, a banshee dancing to singing sands, swimming
nude along the Great Lake shoreline, a berrybrown ondine.

Alice Mabel Gray *(1881–1925), a graduate of the University of Chicago, abandoned her life in Chicago in 1915 to live rough on the shores of Lake Michigan in the sand dunes, where locals referred to her as 'Diana of the Dunes'. She was a tireless eco-campaigner and through her efforts the south shore has largely been preserved as state and national parks instead of being eaten up by the steelmaking industry. Gray claimed city life was not conducive to the advancement of an educated woman. Her ghost is alleged to haunt the park's shores. Each year the town of Chesterton, Indiana holds a beauty pageant called Diana of the Dunes.*

Jane Joritz-Nakagawa

The Lighthouse

Though my eyes are scattered I can hide the emptiness within with a vermilion coat and blue eyelashes. No one will notice that Milton's light has dimmed. I put a verb under every umbrella in case you feel like running. The temple is supposed to mean something but nobody is sure. I thought the cherry blossoms though torn and dirty would last all year but the wind swept through the house knocking over father's funeral photograph. I know I am supposed to stay under a heavy object such as a major appliance. If you pluck a grey hair by its roots doves appear the next day. But that is the ending to last year's story. Though a wound looks like a freshly plowed field I cannot feel responsible for your lost baggage. The truth is I am allergic to everything red and blue, and worry anti-depressants will ruin the sun's melancholia. But I could still watch it from afar while pretending to smile. I hope the sea may be colder than ever and know once I submerge my toe in it it won't come back. Silly to believe birds know the best way to fly to the beach. Skin cancer is the goddess' revenge on the vain and foolish. Just because I've said it doesn't mean it's not true. Sunlight tries to squeeze into every room but fails. The house I grew up in was a dark cave even though my parents were wealthy. I remember the dog was let out every Sunday. How foolish to return. I am more afraid of happiness than I am of the sun's anger. I would like to liven up each house with a piece of rotting fish stolen from the temple. If the lighthouse is painted pink I'll no longer be allergic to it and when the sun resembles caramel latte I'll finally move. I'd suggest birds prefer the sea to the sun but the wind would argue. Even if I am a man so old I can scarcely carry the newspaper to the trash bin. If the drum is beaten with a stick somebody will answer the telephone though my slippers are missing and none of this is actually visible from the lighthouse.

The End of History

Walking outside, hoping the air may be better. The air hops with me. I think of the mail unopened and the unanswered phone. Would it be better to wait in the stale air for the phone or inside the metal box for the mail? Is it better to perfect oneself alone in the dark or desecrate oneself in public? When does the outside become dirty and limiting, muddied by base desire – or is it the inside that is filthy? Though I know I must flee from the machines eating everyone at the office, even though severely admonished for not staying til all my limbs are gone. So with all my limbs, forced to join a doomsday cult where we are asked to sacrifice a limb in order to approximate the masses, yet, I do not, being too selfish (angry?) to give up anything, move alone toward the end of history.

Elizabeth Dodd

Panic

In the dream the panther's paw balanced on its pads like beanbag-based ashtrays from the 1970s, oh my god, like one of those horrific severed hands from an ape cupping a thin line, rising, of smoke. Pan paniscus, pan troglodytes. The fist of a cougar, chopped at the wrist. I woke sweating, lay in the dark thinking of breathing,

recalling a story a friend told me once, how he walked through a canyon creekbed, sandstone walls rising in red-paneled witness, and the cat's tracks, only moments old in the day's brightening light, were filling with water. Like thought.

The king would eat only of the pannick bread, as he had been wont to do. Panicoideae paniceae. Panic grass, panic seed. *Panem depsticum sic facito. Manus mortariumque bene lavato. Which I take to mean, make kneaded bread thus. Wash your hands and trough well*—I lay in the dark remembering lying awake in the dark,

listening. That day Karl had come loping back into camp. 'Hey, I just saw a mountain lion. Let's go look for its tracks in the snow.' Drumbeat of boots crossing over the bridge, the autumn-dry stream. Prints in snowdust, under the trees. Then a blur of speed the color of dry grass.

In the cave of the brainpan, oh the alchemy, the panoply, the high point of the hill where the landscape pans before our gaze, hairs lifting along the neck, as always the world could be watching and finding us wanting, or maybe worse, turning away, turning—

No, no, no.
Lids closed, sunset bloodies the near horizon. Over the lake such a thin pane of ice.

The Problem of Moral Relevance Blooms on North Mesa

Consider the cliff rose.

Along its stalks-becoming-
branches, auxins clot
wherever less light falls.

And, cell by cell, the walls
rise sunward, deciduous dome
in the air's inverted bowl.

Busy old sun, that silent
engine, quoting itself
as it beats the drum.

The chorus is masked
and expectant,
hamartia hung like a cloud
among stars.

One seed lodged in an
angle where cliff isn't
speaking, where dust
huddles in hummocks
against the south face.

Under the skin, hormones murmur,
low, spectral echoes of midsummer light.

Ahhh, fukkit, just make the best of it—

There it is,
    The Good,
sheathed in myelin, maybe,
fountaining outward, rooted in place.

Andrew Forster

The Duddon Valley

After weeks of rain the valley is a swamp,
its floor shimmering scarlet, where grass
is starved of light. The paths have faded,
just one hard winter from wilderness.

Wordsworth loved this place. He came here
in old age, but in mist ghosting the slopes
he saw Coleridge, and others he'd outlived
and felt the earth begin to shrug him off.

We crossed Red Beck and almost slipped
on rain-greased stones, the coldness of the stream
almost visible above it, like vapour,
as it crackles, clear, over cobbles.

Ahead, the slopes which wall this valley
are brown with bracken and patched with snow.
My steps slide off the sparkling white remnants
and I'm forced to take a different route.

The land tilts as if I'd stumbled. Still upright,
sweat prickles my face and my breath
seems to hover ahead of me, out of reach.
These spells are more frequent now.

My own companion is out of sight
around the ridge, focusing on his own ascent.
I lean against a rock until it passes,
then set off again, regain my rhythm.

C. J. Allen

Abandoned Millstones

Then finds its way to now; it has
fallen down a hill. It waits
where is vibrates with what it was.
Haphazardly it rests. Light flits

over rippled stones holed-through
with care but in the end discarded
for what comes next. Nobody knew
what that might be. The weather hurried

on the way that weather does.
The grass grew all the while the world
was busy being somewhere else.
Trees thickened and the branches filled

with leaves. The stones expressed their sense
of effort set aside. Small birds
came and went. Sometimes a rinse
of sun, sometimes the rain. Like words

that no-one uses any more,
the millstones lie beside the path,
undisturbed. A long before
exhales over their aftermath.

WOODEN BOULDER
after the sculpture of the same name by David Nash

If a tree falls or is felled and a man takes a chainsaw
and carves from the trunk what some might consider to be
a boulder-shaped bole which he may or may not plan to use

later for something or other, will this help him to see
who he is or explain what he does to whomever might ask?
And likewise if the man tries to float the thing downstream,

is he dabbling here in the shallows of contradiction,
is he raising the question of how our own lives are criss-crossed
with other, corresponding contradictions?

Then let's say the boulder gets trapped, wedged under a bridge,
and has to be hauled out using a block and an A-frame.
Does this equal the idea's failure, is this an idea

fouled by ambition, or is it perhaps something else
altogether, a secular calling-down of the gods,
an invocation of brute ingenuity?

So as the seasons pass and the wooden boulder rolls
and drifts its way past fields of incurious sheep,
crusted with frost and sometimes glittery

as sunlight glances off its grainy wetness,
are we talking here, albeit conceptually,
albeit in the time-lapsed tongue of nature,

about beauty's connection to mutability?
And as it rocks and sinks and bobs its way along
in the tidal expanse of a salt-marsh and out to sea,

is it part of a larger loneliness travelling through
the landscape, or is its going meant to be
no more than a method and means to set things free?

Frances Presley

Oak Change

The oak has changed its nature and this is called the Oak Change. Hitherto oaks had grown from seed within existing woods, but with few exceptions this ceased in the twentieth century. They were supposed to hold their own in the plot, as part of a densely worded argument and the interjection of many different, though similar, and invasive voices. Anything else was regarded as being contrary and self seeking. He had not noticed that methods of inscription had changed in the twentieth century, with the gradual elimination of the curving loop which led up to the first person pronoun. Oak now grows freely from acorn almost anywhere – heathland, farmland, railway land (although these anywheres are diminishing) – except within existing woods. Old photographs show a dense cluster of family members reliant on the spread skirt of the female lap, although some females sit perfectly upright. There is no trace of the adult males. This was the pattern he had wanted to recreate.

To sum up the main points of the argument, the oak changed its nature and this was not transcribed in his manual of fruit trees. It is disconcerting that a common tree should violate the Principle of Uniformity – that its present behaviour should furnish an interpretation of the past – and there has been much conjecture as to its cause. The most plausible reason is the introduction from America of oak mildew, a fungus disease first noticed in 1908 that rapidly spread to every deciduous oak in Europe.

The best of her men and most of her money had
disappeared in the mud of Europe
The mildew has little effect on oaks growing in the open – but it may be death to an oakling in a wood struggling against shade.

My parents were not easily dismayed, I was their eighth offspring

In the next generation, however, there were principles which no longer seemed to apply, such as the assumed lack of communication between the male and its offspring.

We'll never rear them, mother

He may have had some awareness of the change, as he gestured at a clearing in the woods, and thought that most suitable for a sapling. The National Trust did not agree, although they rarely check the spread of sweet chestnut, laurel, rhododendron, and other opportunists, due to the absence of tied cottagers.

We deal with trees as actors in the play

That it should come to this, Horatio

their shades have become our anywhere

Pippa Little

BELNAHUA

Slate shore:
like the shucked-off wings of geese
slippery, wind-honed quills
click beneath our feet.

The quarry falls in,
stars wheeze blue,
cannot burn
in a hearthless house:

who sleeps here now
who hears in
seagulls' mewling
echo of chisel and hammer?

Where to split down through the slate's grain,
how to cleave clean,
plane a life's clattering
into some kind of pattern –
all our knowing
has been stolen from this place.

Ruth Padel

MEETING THE LEMMING

None of the story is true. Hurtling over the edge
(listen, says the dark) we repeat it on Facebook over
and over, divinity lies in shutting our eyes.
White Wilderness faked the myth with domestic
lemmings, screwed out of Eskimo children,
flown from Hudson Bay and put to race on a snow-
covered turntable. Tight camera angles, what they do
to denial: turn a handful of pets to a mass mob-run
over tundra. An ice-rink. Then Disney's film crew
threw them off a cliff. Over they go
you can see them on celluloid, falling through
the silver aspic of 1950s air, a lake of dying rodents
longhaired as Tuppenny the runaway guinea-pig
in *The Fairy Caravan;* like hamsters my brother kept
and kept losing through that hole under the bath
in the house where black hollyhocks grew high
as the bedroom window. That same brother
who caught frostbite on a mountain in Norway,
lingering to inspect the tricolor silks – black,
chestnut and white – of a single lemming.

Em Strang

The Woodchester Beast

Sundown and the men have been waiting
all day for the news, drinking pints of ale
in the Hare & Hounds, lisping about the big
cat, her broad head, her teeth and claws.
Somewhere in the soft woods, deep
in the purple fuzz of trees and brambles,
the big cat is prowling, each paw
the size of a woman's face.
Nobody has seen her by day, but as light
dims and the birds murmur to roost,
experts report sightings of a shadowy
figure in and out of the tree-line, something
loping with intent, biding time at the body
of water near Nailsworth Common,
before slipping into the absolute
black of binocular cases and lens caps.
When they found her, she was ripped
at the belly, guts torn out in one swift
manoeuvre, head mangled. Someone
said it was the work of a big cat
but the woman had been violated, legs
akimbo, blood seeping from her sex.

The Place
After Janet Frame

The place where the cows licked
their mineral block,
teased hay from the cratch in the hock-deep mud
is gone.

You know the place –
in the field with its back to the world
beyond the beech trees,
the bludgeoned ground.

Now I remember
these things in blood and bone,
in rain-pocked skin where water continues to seep
indelibly in.

Parsnip

i

We
wash
off
the
mud
to
reveal
tap
roots
of
infinite
tenderness,
feelers
reaching
from
body
to
earth.

ii

And the locals said they'd never seen anything like it,
that there was something infra dig about the fact
that it was as big as the kitchen table, lying there
like a slain beast on a Sunday afternoon in January.
If you'd wielded a spade you'd know how it felt
as you heaved and hacked at the earth, loosened
the wet, cloying soil from the off-white flesh
of the thing. Some say it was hexed, that the blade
that first struck was a fated blade of a fated man,
that from then on his crops would grow
thorns so big and sharp that the man would bleed
for days, hands like a surgeon's or worse.

It was the inn-keeper's daughter who cooked it.
She peeled its skin one afternoon as the snow
came on. She chopped it up and set it to boil
in twenty silver pans of salty water.
If you'd stirred the brew you'd know how it felt
as the heat rose and the heart softened,
like a man sleeping in his endless bed
or the relief of a starving village,
soup bowl in every bony hand.

Jennifer Wallace

My Eyes Look Everywhere: Needles and Neon, a Few Squirrels

Sometimes I withdraw from the city. Not kneeling toward
the moss rock by the sea. And all the while the seasons rush over
    the sidewalks: petals, colored leaves, the neighbors'
footfalls. Crows flock to the parks, gather in the trees. The
    closeness of otherness is touching but not to be touched.

I am asked: "Do you think living in the city has something
to do with your poems about thought?" As in: will a place
    that bends the rain make things more clear? As in: a man
talked to his son about the bird's obsessive flight: in and out
    of the chimney's narrow passage...a dumb
flight that must be undertaken: 'It is deeper than your father, boy.'

On street corners: a handshake, fist, words exchanged.
The fears excited by such intimacies. Are momentary.
    Replaced by: "Which bus is mine?" And we are on our way.
To the parks and gardens, which present an illusion of access.

Today at the corner, a lady dressed all in green...
new-leaf green...green shoes, even, against the concrete curb.
    We were looking for a bus in the rain. Pelting rain,
all over those shoes. Impenetrable, natural rain. She carried
    Jehovah's pamphlet. We were looking.

I WANTED TO CHANGE MY NAME

I wanted to change my name, find a remote island
off the Newfoundland coast. The only way to get there
would be by boat, and only I would send it and only
on occasion. I'd be a friend of gannets. Emerson's protégé.

Time would exist as it should: tidal and thick
as a forest. I'd be historical. A spinster on a bright day
clipping asters outside a clapboard shed, my graying
hair wild with wind. In November, I'd split wood and
welcome the kid from town who'd deliver my mail.
I'd catch my fish. I'd be a kingdom, an ecology.

How could I have known that my arrival would
build itself on contradiction. Instead of ocean: murder;
exhaust, not flowers. In this metropolis: all the homes
with the name "Stranger" carved on their doors.

There is a grammar etched in the mind's bone.
A topography that can be counted on. It might erode—
with time and weather—but beauty and ugliness
run in its gullies. With more or less volume. At will, if willed.

Fiona Russell

At the Old Buchts

An emptiness, like a church forsaken,
its sporadic services done.

Rows of rippled tin pegged to posts,
stained the death of autumn brackens.

Skiffs of fleece, beads of keel,
memories gathered, pinned to pens.

Wooden wicket gates sag, asleep in the shedder,
reliving white legs rattling off tin,

hurdling of hoggs, hirds roaring *hoors!*
in booming bass and tenors tones,

yapping of collies coaxing yowes,
all echoing tongues lost, as if in mist.

For Rachael,

May the tide bring you inspiration, the sun warmth and love, and the breeze memories of shared times.

Fiona Russell x

Dod Fell
After Owen Sheers

One touch of nature makes the whole world kin.
William Shakespeare

Unlike the hunters who dropped
bones of beasts on her unhallowed chest
we are spurned by the questions
of the answers we have always known.

From the nipple on her heights,
a sharp frost piercing her torso
to the secrets that she hides
without movement in her shoulders.

The flatness of her skin,
all smooth rock and leaching damp,
sulking beneath a sharp sun, a gregarious body
gathering the Cheviots in.

Her north-south cheeks, one bright, one sullen,
hers, a formality without boundaries,
her airiness, as weathered tomes
of a well-kent kin.

Wee Byre, After the Storm

Last week her gable end blew out,
left fallen bricks to lie in broken ranks.
Her ribs exposed now wheeze and heave
weathering in another westerly wind.

Two ropes, a cable hang, swish wind-swing.
Night-light, an owl's hushed white wings.
Long gone the clatter of three-legged beech on cobbles,
the squirts of midwinter milk kissing shiny steel.

No hens cluck, foxed, empty dust-mesh pen hangs open.
Collie dogs quiet, no howling, no hirds, no whistles leach,
just a roaring river forever rushing past,

where winter dipper song cuts a deep red sunset
sweetening the simmering stab of a harpoon frost.

Roger Mitchell

Undersong

The garden wall project had a unique advantage: it could be carried on for an hour or two, dropped for a day or two—or a week or a month—and then picked up again.
                    Helen and Scott Nearing, *The Good Life*

i
There's a common yellowthroat close by
and a grosbeak cranks its 'churleywallop'
in the draw. I underlined the poems
of John Clare one year looking for words
to describe something. I was hoping
he would know what the something was.
The garden goes quietly to its death
each year. Last night something topped
the seedling chard I planted
only last week. I love to water.
I would almost rather water
than write, mow than think. It feels right,
doing as well as being done with.
'It could be carried on for an hour
or two, dropped for a day or two—
or a week or a month...' I stopped
reading right there. That was enough.
It was something you did forever,
your piece of it, without ever
finishing it. We haven't yet found
the beginning, so why assume there was one?

ii
I took them from the bird poems
thinking, I suppose, that birds
would make him warble, too, or veer
just enough away from things
to make them clear.
'The little sinky foss', for instance,
that streaks the moors where the snipe hides,
or the 'sweeing bough' on which
the happy white throat sways.
The mingling of 'crimpled leaves
with furze and ling'.
And when he needed it, to 'sluther' down
and disappear, as though to sluth
was what it sounded like, to drag
your feather through the slime,
to hide your gorgeousness
as though it was its own enemy.
And the flood-washed river banks
where bared roots 'crankle' back
into the bank to keep a tree
from crashing in the wash.
All he wanted came from a hedge
where birds 'court and build'
and sing what he called their 'under song',
their song of being other
than it seemed to passing strangers,
those who had their own netherness
and, as he might have put it,
plucked it from the furze and ling
and made from it an everlasting,
by which it should be understood,
an unfinishing, thing.

In a Field

Here's where the spring runoff passes through,
flowing into a terrace of small ponds
made by a beaver. Two bitterns nest there,
and a nightly aria of peeping frogs
eases us into sleep. It's been raining
every day. When the clouds rush at us
over the mountains, we can almost time
the slap of the first drop. The streams quiver
and swirl with the excess. We stand and watch
biceps of brown water curl over the rocks.

Last night we went down into the village
to look at the river, down where they built
the first mill. The stone foundation still hugs
the inside bank of the river's curve.
Here was the heart of the original
settlement. Today, fishermen cast around
in the pools and washes, or if it's hot,
people sit in the natural tubs,
hammer themselves into numbness
under an avalanche of drumming water.

One evening, up the hill in back of us,
miles from the village, where there are now woods,
some of them newly logged, beyond the last
two or three small camps buried in the gloom,
where the land crests and the first ridge reaches
toward the height of the whole eastern side
of the gouge made by the last glacier
retreating into the Arctic,
we came into a meadow of tall grass
where two crabapples blossomed on the far side

and almost hidden under the alders
and poplars, a rough wall of stones someone
had dragged out of the way straggled along
its edge. Nothing remains of the plain life
this short meadow called into being. No
stone tells us the year or the day, the name,
of any event, person, birth or death.
All we know is that people came to this place,
and when they left, the trees grew to the edge
and, as though in dumb homage, stopped.

In our own field, the place at the back
where they put the machines that broke for good.
It's turned into a rough museum
of ideas that once worked but now look
exotic or quaint. The pitched bottles and cans
fill up with mud. Broken toys, rusted
wire, most of an old Ford pickup. We're
not sure where we are in this gradual
collision of histories and landscapes,
collage of molted lives and livelihoods,

but the fox that hunts here often is glad
for the birds and the field mice. Likewise,
the hawks and owls. Though we know that once
this valley wound through a thickness of pines
and cedars higher than anything left,
it's with something like regret that we watch
the field slowly erase the marks of those
who cleared it and, to farm it, moved a wall
of huge boulders into place along the back
with no better tools than they who,
thousands of years ago, raised the pyramids.

Paul Lindholdt

BROODING SEASON

Further and further out the partridge flees
peeping, feigning a hurt wing, luring the dog
from the hidden nest at the field's edge,
landing on the ground only long enough
to give the old retriever hope, open-mouthed,
bounding, oblivious to our shouted commands.
We've come in June, brooding season, wrong
to have brought the big Labrador trained
for the chase, lost now in the genetic code
to capture and kill although the season's closed.

If we were puritans prone to morality tales
we might say the dog loses itself to instinct
every day while we yield ourselves only in the fall.
But now we're living closely in the moment,
rooting for the partridge to escape and it does,
it dupes the dog, this predator we've bred to doze
at our feet, and our finest philosophies can't
subtract the tension from the scene or sketch it
in ethical shades. From the border of the field
we human beings see a bird fly up and out of sight.

Alistair Peebles

Provided

early as you said
the dung smells
of spring

fields all day
greening
out of snow

evening
oldearthopening
telling all I am

and mild tonight
the cries of birds
the many notes of rain

Heather linties, hundreds
Maeshowe to Skara Brae, 23rd February 2010

Sycamore in bud,
leaves crumpled into frost
– a winter of east winds

  almost immediately
  clouds cover Hoy

codes of the highway –
face the oncoming traffic
be alert for the nod

  drivers on the side roads,
  still pedestrians, wave

where the waters meet,
between sheets of ice
– widgeon, dunters, swans

  feeding time –
  four nosing the air

the loch overcast,
potched like weathered agate,
turbined hills a-glinting

  a slab roof very
  neatly edged with hail

ontheonehand, ontheother
this ring of stones
those shining blades

    widdershins at Brodgar
    sun breaking through

land of the living
land of the dead
– which is which?

  mute by the fence,
  uncertain too

the flocks, the flocks
the noise of the flocks
stops

  over the Lyde
  a half moon, pale and rising

from a hilltop henge –
who's that speeding past Craya?
what's that speck on the Flow?

  half the world at a glance
  your back out of the wind

she tells of a friend
loves surfing so much
he lives in a van

  new houses, new fences
  new folks in old places

heather linties, hundreds,
sing the broken track
a whole aisle

    behind me again
    before me again

if being on earth
is finding ways to heaven,
this was one

    some topography's
    more local

snow is and is not
there is sunlight and shade
distant showers are beautiful

    bedsheets, lilac,
    lifting on the breeze

a gap in the hills
for the bottle-blue ocean
the steady horizon

    barking, barking,
    barking,

the phone box
loud
and silent

    sunlit garage door
    open on a neat bench

Margaret Tait,
Mary Graham Sinclair –
Bolex, Fergie, 'some beauty'

    stabs piled,
    wires taut, waiting

feathered for spring,
the flash and pleep
of a snipe

    that head-turning
    drift of slurry

bales, sprawled at the fence –
but here she comes, beaming,
straight from the salon

    the beach half-white,
    criss-crossed with footprints

miles to visit
these tidy rooms,
neighbour-like

    back through the years
    and years, we drive on home.

And so

it starts again with cutting ground,
turf eased up and soil turned,
on a February morning,
bright, *for a wonder*, and warm.
The blades mirror a dark earth,
well kent and kind,
for scarce a stone drags out
to snag or blunt them:
sheer forms, heirlooms often,
hauled inch-fine by experts, all
on their mettle at the Match today,
at Vola, Grimeston, Harray.

In ploughing time, generations gone,
strips uncoil between beast and man,
or now, between a man
and the beasts coming after.
It's lonely, sometimes, up in the cab,
a public office for one – but here's
company, competition, cups of tea,
and prizes, a write-up, a yarn…

'Vola'? from 'vole'? I'm wondering,
remembering earlier,
when I'd parked at the lochside
in a freezing fog, and trailed
among the standing stones,
and over the bitten grass, so lately
slabbed with ice, and over
the tunnels the voles had made
– a network like veins,
discovered by the thaw.

I'd been thinking of a friend,
of the photographs she'd taken there,
of myself taking photographs now,
and then her man came to mind,
telling me, this winter,
walking – *oh the walking helps* –
into town, into work, how he'd
stopped, and heard them
under the snow, squeaking
and scratching...

You can't be sure, of course,
where any of this is going,
day by day – but then a day
comes round, when an hour
after standing by the frozen loch,
thinking of friends, admiring voles,
watching swans drift back and forth
in their own clear path, you find
yourself, for *it's turned out fine*,
in shirtsleeves, among the chiels
and tractors tilting over the old land
               – a breath of vapour,
sunlit for a moment, rising from the loam.

dee Hobsbawn-Smith

Driving the Mares
for Jon and Andrea

Look at me. You think I don't understand?
What is the animal
if not passage out of this life?
                        Louise Glück

i

In spring, endure muddy lanes ripening, drive to where the mares wait to have their dusty coats shone into honey gloss, forelocks disheveled from their straw-padded barn, tails parading with each stroke of the curry comb.

Eyes, private waterplaces. Ears, open-hinged pivot-tufts capture the morning's music made by congregating chickadees, flying through the cracking light of spring as the air holds its breath.

The harness upon their withers, Girth. Crupper. Hame. Breeching. Ancient words from countries in love with horses, meanings lost, then found, as lines untangle themselves, align massive ribs, haunches, bellies, string leather reins through blind metal eyes. *Look at me. You think I don't understand?*

ii

Shake the reins and coax them, the plough's long shanks waiting in the sun. Back them into place, quick slow quick slow quick, slide breeching around hips, traces into imaginary lockstep of eight hooves, their legs engage, pistons dinning across the yard.

In the field during high summer, hay tumbles behind the haymow, falling in languid sheaves behind their heels. Stop for lunch, drop

the reins, free the mares to graze, velvet mouths on burgeoning
timothy and brome, the truth of generosity that defines
What is the animal.

iii

Follow them all year, leather reins instead of a rough voice to
curb them. Their wild-maned filly-daughters running in the
grass, mothers and aged aunts, gray mares now, their running
days done, those years, the haymow rusting in the fields.

What are they to me, this massive movement, this certainty on four
legs? What they sing, what they slowly dance, what they cleave
to, bridle and bit and throat latch, why their willingness? What
do they give so freely, to me, ploughing my own uncertain field,
if not passage out of this life?

Hejira

i

Late summer, the sky
is barking like a carnie
as I drive beneath its high blue tent.
Shuswap Lake crowded with houseboats, all
their windows glazed with fire-eater's silver.
Time is a juggler's clock I don't unwind.

Perfect summer in my trunk, two cases
of peaches, fingerprints on each golden cheek
like a farmer's goodbye kiss. As I pass
the ranks of tree trunks tarnished
by forest fire, up the long valley road, I hear
a carousel of vacationers
long before I see you on the marina dock.

Amid their raucous celebrations,
we climb aboard the houseboat
pointing northward through the channel.
We leave the circus lights behind, the lake
a melted shadow beneath the moon.

ii
At Anstey Arm, two aspen trees stand sentinel,
the pine forest silent, waiting
behind them. We wake early,
make peach pie for breakfast,
eat above the pooling water, warm slices
dripping amber, sticky hands we wash in the lake
like paws. A bear
appears from behind the shining trees,
rears on his hind legs, waves us off his ground.

iii
The beach is a sandy palm gesturing
at vanishing rocks and rivulets. We drop anchor,
our bare feet padding down the wooden gangplank,
leave our footprints in the smooth shingle.

I see in your face the explorer's dream
of the uncharted, your hope reflected
in the stream we follow. In a shallow pond,
we see four salmon, ghosts,
water brown and green upon translucent ribs,
almost motionless. They know it's not
the unknown we have found, but home.

Flood Plain

You fear running dry, the ghost dust
of '30s drought,
its desiccation—words and life might dry right out of you
before you tap your own artesian
water table.

Dredge up last summer,
before you decided to move back,
listening to your mother in the shower,
a child of the dustbowl,
two minutes in and out.

When the shower abruptly
turns into a trickle, your heart
quickens—*the pump the pump*—
and you move quickly
to shut it off,
imagining the pipe running
across the yard, from house to pump-house,
the tunnel's seventy-foot plunge to water,
its uncertain flow.

This year the water table is above ground.
You live lakeside, an unexpected generosity
in dryland, fifteen acres inundated,
no alfalfa or barley seeded this spring,
the south field drowning four feet deep.

You use your grandfather's rusted
Model A as a gauge,
water now six inches from its roof—it floats
where last year, cattle grazed.

Morning walks take you
two hundred yards east, three hundred west, before you meet
the waves. Inland waves. Who ever thought the wind
would carry them so far from the Pacific,
these crests and whitecaps that chase across
your land?

You rush to write each day, capture the flood
at its peak, green mallards bobbing, head up head down head up,
buffleheads and coots, their staccato call a rapid-fire song,
the Mormon tabernacle choir of frogs, bellowing
from reeds and floating lengths of wood.

From your second-storey studio, you inhale the funk
of algae bloom, marshiness pungent as duck feet,
ferns and fiddleheads, cattails uncoiling.

Black snail shells crunch
beneath your boots, coagulating in heavy mud,
its viscous cling between your toes. You find egg shells
cracked, outgrown, ducklings in shipping lanes
                        behind their mothers,
learning to skip like pebbles across the lake.

The lake brings you gifts— last year's abandoned
tractor tires washed to shore,
a metal fuel tank logjammed on the driveway's
verge. Yesterday you saw a beaver,
its tail cutting a wedge across the gloss,
wondered where he sailed in from,
all these years of small ponds.

Watch the waves, coming plain into view
their lace-edged emerald duckweed surging,
receding with the wind, and you wonder
what the world will bring you next.

Rody Gorman

Air an Doirling mu Dheireadh

Is an aimsir a' fàs blàth, siud an deigh
Ris a' mhol 's an fhaoilinn fo reothadh buan
A rinn an gleidheadh le chèile 's an dìon
Uair a' glanadh às. Is doineann a' sloisreadh
Air an doirling mu dheireadh an fhoghair,
A' ghailleann a' mùrach gu domhainn san eighre
Gus an èirich an leaghadh is an t-aiteamh
'S an ùir ga fuasgladh is ga leagail na broinn
'S a' teàrnadh na h-aon lochan dhan Chuan Siar.
Is oir an eilein a' cnàmh is a' briseadh
Na bruan is a' dol falamh, balbh fhèin.
Is an fheadhainn a ghabh tàmh mu na machraichean,
Fiù 's ged a thuiteadh sìde nan seachd sian,
'S mu na gearraidhean ag imrich à baile.

On the Last Pebblygulfstreampeninsulasound at Last

with the epochseasontimeweather wastegrowbecoming
seagreen-fieldwhiteflowerwarm there's the ice on the
poleshingle and the hollwbeachford under permafrost
which keeps them both together and roofprotects them
one hourtime. and a powerstorm washdashing on the last
pebblygulstreampeninsulasound at last at the end of the
autumnharvest, the snow-stormblast downdigging deep
into the ice until the melting and proofthawing risehappen
and the bodyfiresoil loosens and falls in its wombside
and afterbirthdescends like a pisspond into the Atlantical
Western Oceanbay. and the edge of the island bone-
eroding and burstbreaking in woundthrustfragments and
gobecoming poorscarce-empty and dumbsilent. and those
who sleepdwelled by the lowlandfarmbeachmachair, even if
the temps of the seven elements were to befall, and by the
cutgrazinghead-lands, flitting from townvillagefarmhome

Susie Patlove

Divertimento
after Amy Dryansky

The thread that runs through all things
        is what, a filament? A strand of my own seeing?
A pulsating line curving from tree to tree,
        and down into the dark cathedrals of stone?

Did I say seeing? I meant knowing
        because the pulsation of the world
        falls asleep in my body
        settles into a silent undoing
        the river that winds its song
        through the woods falls quiet
        and all that might be heard
        lives outside the closet of my days

When I said heard I meant sensed
        because we can absorb this world
        as it moves through the body
        still I ignore the damp smell
        of decay that floods the forest
        and being blinded by the yellow
        flower of a finch I miss
        the elastic pitch of its song

When I say elastic I *mean* that
        because the line through all things
        stretches curves jumps back
        the way streaks of sunlight
        rake the winter woods
        until a halting spring
        begins its long climb out of soil

I say climb but in some ways I mean float
> because waking up is effortless
> sound is ever present
> and what can be heard
> travels down the bones of a body
> opening chamber after chamber
> where long white curtains blow
> in the wide wind of the world

I say wind but perhaps it is a kind of breath
> the in and out of one universe
> pulsating through stars and cells
> back and forth between joy and sorrow
> allowing us to travel here
> as we balance left foot then right
> on the thin rail that stretches
> forward then falls back behind

I say rail but I know
> no such line runs out ahead
> there is nothing permanent
> no known place to put tomorrow's step
> time doesn't stretch out
> but surrounds us in the broad
> call of our senses—it breathes
> slowly through the sharp shoot
> of knotweed and travels with passion
> down the tumbling river rocks

David Chorlton

What Comes

When you live close to nature, you take what comes.
Tom Beatty, Miller Canyon, Arizona

It might be a Lucifer hummingbird
whose gorget shines magenta
against apples ripening
on trees in August's orchard
that you see, or else

a family from Oaxaca
who made it this far and chose the wild
canyon after crossing over
and who stop
when you encounter them,
frightened as the ocelot

a dog treed here in spring.
If you look the other way
to let them pass
you'll notice how the cliff wall
seems to hang
between the sky and the oaks

while at the saddle
between two peaks
aspens are absorbed by clouds
one day and by smoke
on another. When what comes

is fire, it is never in the forecast.
It just begins
and strips
a mountain to the bone.
When you live where the border
between good weather and bad

is harder to cross
than the one between countries,
it might be the black flood you hear
washing away the thrush's call
and taking back
everything the golden days

delivered. What comes is yours
to keep; as much a part of you
as the shiver in the blade
is of the axe.

Wolf Politics

The wolf, having insufficient vocabulary
beyond the calls that leave a trail
of silver in the air, cannot understand
when it is spoken of as being expendable.
The wolf is a social animal

and has no room in its pack for division
between parties. It takes
what it needs but never has anything
left to collect interest. Wolf time

is the present moment; making platforms
or agendas irrelevant. To the wolf,
a kill is never veiled
in political justification. It does not
first deliberate, and afterwards
pretend remorse. A wolf

doesn't know its range
is disappearing until
there isn't anywhere to go
when it runs to the end of its breath.
Wolves have not romanticized their freedom,

they just hold on
to as much of it as they can.
It isn't easy

when politics comes down
to trading them away in a deal
from which nobody
can vote them back to life.

Les Murray

High Speed Trap Space

Speeding home from town
in rainy dark. For the narrowness
of main roads then, we were hurtling.
A lorry on our tail, bouncing, lit our mirrors,
twinned strawberries kept our lights down

and our highway lane was walled
in froth-barked trees. Nowhere to swerve –
but out between trunks stepped an animal,
big neck, muzzle and horns, calmly gazing
at the play of speed on counter-speed.

Its front hooves up, planted on the asphalt
and our little room raced on to a beheading
or else to be swallowed by the truck's high bow.
No dive down off my seat would get me low
enough to escape the crane-swing of that head

and its imminence of butchery and glass.
But it was gone.
The monster jaw must have recoiled
in one gulp to give me my survival.
My brain was still full of the blubber lip,

the dribbling cud. In all but reality
the bombstroke had still happened.
Ghost glass and blurts of rain still showered
out of my face at the man
whose straining grip had had

to refuse all swerving.

Paul Kingsnorth

The Testament of Edward Abbey

I rode the rapids here before the dam,
before the place filled up with people
mewling like cats for the warmth of four walls.
I saw black bears by the dozen in those woods.
It's lumber now. Don't ask me.
I was in the War, I saw
what Men will do.

You should have caught this place before
the freeways and the missile silos,
before the Big Boys fucked it up.
Well, they'll come for me. It's late,
the monster grows, I owe the Earth
a body. Take me when it's time
out to the desert, where we drank
that night to the old sad Spirit.
Dig a hole they'll never find.

And may you live to see it fall,
to see the lumbermen and the miners,
the candidates and the tax collectors
choke on their planks and ashes.
And may you see the fish return
when they bring Glen Canyon down.
Fare you well, then. Ride the rivers,
take your beer cans home.
Struggle like a fly in the Machine's oil.
Be of good cheer. Count the stars.
Keep running.

From the Fjord

Look now look
I promise
this is not an argument

this is a high-sided mountain
green with wood wights and lines of great red birds
ridiculous in their understanding invisible
in their known place. This is peace
for those who come from outside war
for the beasts of the night for the puma
and the unthinking hawk.

I promise
I am not making a point I have nothing
to sell you this is not a demonstration of
fitness for purpose of the still
before the Fall or of the coming after
this is not politics there is no end.
This is only the wildness of being
shored up by eroding bones black with decay
cut through with beauty painful to come to
impossible to turn from in time.

Jane Routh

The Teachings of *Strix aluco*

First you must learn stillness.
You must learn to wait inside shadow:
even your breath must not disturb
the air around you. Forget time. Forget
the body – be nothing but eyes:
a last blackbird fruitless on the lawn,
a pair of rooks giving up on the day
as day gives itself up to the night.

Clear your mind of shades of grey.
Dusk is not, as you think, continuum.
There is a moment when it is day; after it, night.
You will learn this is not the same as when electric lights
click on in the milking parlour across the valley. No,
night comes always later than you expect.
Study the light. Make a judgment of your own:
this is your second lesson.

Watch.   Watch.
If you have judged right,
out of the fold in the cypress tree,
out of that cleft between day and night
in one swift unfolding downward swoop,
          I:
one wingbeat and your world is dark.
Watch.   Watch as well as you can and you will lose me.
You will never be able to say where I went, what I do.
This is the lesson you won't ever learn:
how much there is you can never know.

The Private Life of *Lepus lepus*

AT HIS TOILET

If he had not been so particular...

the meadow still, morning light in the dew
Nothing moves
a black   flickering

something about his left ear
he scratches scratches scratches
with his hind leg

a quick change of sides,
right leg behind right ear to even things up
then flicking the left again and again

He sits up

Paddles his front feet in the dew
rubs them together, rubs and rubs
then washes his face

Paddles in the dew
rubs his paws together and together
and washes his face

Did I see him spit on his hands?

SLEEPING

Only because I already knew…

there: in the slight south-facing dip
before the meadow curves down to the wood

that last molehill in the run,
the soil slightly lighter (ears flat-packed along his back)

Day after day in his form
blades of grass just so

Is he dead?
Watch

sometimes a deep breath
– the molehill heaves

Day after day
I watch at the upstairs window

ABOUT HIS BUSINESS

Hare gone dandying
down in the woods
His fields, not mine

I can see where he lay

O I want to walk out
in his field
and touch his form

I know every blade
could walk straight there
three paces left of those rushes

BETRAYED

After the gale, making notes:
which trees to be felled, fences
to be tightened, and a short cut

unintended
close by his form
its deep slot, angle of thigh

Old man hare lolloping by
along the berm
treats me to his disregard

He saw me
          looking
Won't be back

Mark-making

– You've made your mark, he says,
nodding at woodland I planted thirty years back.

The hedge that he's laying is almost a woodland itself:
he's dropped thirty- and forty-foot trees both sides of the line,

reckon's no one's touched it this last fifty year.
He shows me an ash trunk, the rings that he counted:

I bet the thin one near the centre was that dry year, '77,
and count back from the bark, but he says it was '76

that was dry and '84 that was wet: he'll never forget
the length of the grass that year, how no one could get in the hay

– the talk about making one's mark, networking and fame
tossed aside with the brash for what keeps us grounded.

From down here on his land, the woodland I planted
looks as if it's always been there. I like this view:

birch trunks that much whiter in front of Scots pine,
a few ash crowns breaking the skyline beyond.

My woodland. His hedgerow.
– Isn't it the other way round? Don't these things mark us?

I've backtracked, but he knows what I mean, pauses
then tells me to pace out the length of a brier he's just woven in.

Kathleen Jones

RAVEN GOES TRAVELLING

i

Raven puts on his sky-skin
the colour of midnight
to perch on the house-pole

his spread wings trailing
the feathered edges of the pine forest
his beak a scoop for the ocean.

He has left his voice
with the long-eyed spirit of the sea

and under the wave
it calls far back
through the memory of water
the salt coast rasp
in its octave

singing stories of stolen sisters
bone hooks
and seal babies and
the flayed skins of geese and marten
as blankets for Shamen...

'No one else sings it like this
for it was I who dreamed it myself.'

This is the raven travelling.
The one who cannot be named.

ii

The raven auditions for a mate.
She is curious, eager
to be convinced by his footwork.

The raven jumps – one charcoal claw
to the other. Left. Right.

A shrug of the wing, flight
feathers spread like the span of a hand.

                              A quick
jink of the head, jye-necked
beak to beak. Left. Right.

Raven is pitch perfect
jump, jink, shrug – and then

the brag of his wing
over her.

iii

Raven in his tuxedo.
Black tie. Reflective shades.
The magpie look.
Raven is Celebrity. His hunger
is bigger than the world.

He has rolled up the mountains and lakes
and the forests like a pancake
and eaten them. He has sold
the sea otter for its pelt, felled
the yellow cedar, swallowed
the coho and chinook
the red cod and the black cod.

Traded the whales in the ocean
for gospel and guns and secret
accounts in the Cayman islands
to tempt the woman at his elbow
raven-haired, a dress of silver scales
as supple as salmon skin, the stars of the universe
on her fingers and swinging from her ears.   And
he is still hungry.

iv

Crow's cousin
black in the blue alphabet
hung in the thorn hedge
by the neck – jet
claws still clutching
tail feathers a dark rainbow
in the spectrum of mourning
one eye open
the long beak parted –

*'I am everything I see and
I am this too.'*

He has left his sky-skin
for the flies.

The Islands of the Light

This is where East is
where the sun harbours
ready to lift above
the glass horizon
still reflecting the after-
glow of the West.

Freckles of dark
on the silver skin of the sea
no more than you can count
on the double span of your hands.
A green bloom, blurring
into focus the rock, creek, forest,
a glittering scatter of water.

Then the rotted log houses
and the bay, excavated
by the archaeology of light.

Watch, how it alters perspective
drawing a line, flat
then elevated; how the sea
looks curiously level from here;
how the white underbelly
of the orca, seems like the white
curve of the waves' lip, where
the Canoe People endlessly paddle
and the whales throw themselves
on the shore as a gift.

The Hunters

They came with heavy weapons
black-bound, clasped in brass.
New words. A dark catechism
like a stone in the mouth
to hamper the tongue.

Not with the sap-wine of the birch and pine
Nor with the pot-latch dance to celebrate the sun
Not with the blood of your sworn enemies
Nor with the sister of your father's wife
Nor clothed in the skin of animals

but dressed in linsey-wolsey, twill,
brown cord, small clothes of flannel
next to the skin, next to the soul
the virtuous linen of the Sabbath fast.
Superior Shamen, dressed in black

with hat and satchel, move in for the kill,
bring trading posts, fish factories,
a plain room for the spirits of the dead.
The timber mortuary pole
with its carved figure of a man.

'*No one else sings it like this/ for it was I who dreamed it myself*' (p.148) Pamich, trans. Kwatnialka, 1903, quoted A.L. Kroeber, *Seven Mojave Myths* (University of California Press, 1948).

Susan Richardson

The White Doe

As transformations go,
this has no more daunt than the suddening
of blood and breasts. It's horizontal at its best –
belly hammocked between four legs
instead of back-trapped, compliant-wifing.

Though my hands have hooved,
they're now attuned to fungus-rub and moss.
My teeth are flossed heatherly,
I splursh through burns
and I've learned to ask the sun to fondle-flank
after twenty-one dark-cursed years.
Birch bark tonguing me.
Crossbills beaking pine seeds tweakily from cones.
Ground-smelling rowan, berrily with otterness.
Ear-twitch to a cracklish sound –
worker ants nest-mounding.
All such a gorgeous –
not even the flies round my side-head eyes
can undeer me now.

At last I can be forgettish –
no more bracelets, grammar, manners,
standard lamps, strip lights.
No more room-fug of stew
and my stale mother's breath.
No more lonelies and youfreaking.
No more curtains, shutters, blinds.

Instead, my hind-mind's ferned
with ancient memories of wolf
and the urge to neverstill.
Though the man I was meant to wed
turns hunter,
I will out-wood him.
For an unlife in the unlight
has taught me slinkness,
and how to happyeverafter
when I tellme tales.

Jane McKie

The Rife

Primary school children prod
measuring sticks at it, and—surprise!—
it prods back, wallop of water, spring
from the dribble of river mud.
There is laughter.
The water comes from nowhere,
hangs for a moment before it falls,
flocked-mirror-water, stretched-mirror-
water, a frying pan of reflected light.
There is no simple origin, no fish's
fountain, no motor thrown into reverse.
Just a window that opens out
of sumpy air, a caesura
through which life can resume its flow.

Beaching of a Pod of Whales at Loch Carnan

Those things that languish in the shallows
are telling their stories, truthful and slow,
muted through water. It takes generations.

Above Benbecula, in less than a second, their spirits burn off.

Nancy Holmes

Suburban Summer Ode

i. night

every few seconds air seeds the lungs
ploughs more dark into the clouds
gets more crusted with dog barks, cricket creaks, car rushes
trees tug o' war wind mass and shadow
while blue TV light shivers at the windows
I thought I told my own story but as the dreams
blow in, they carry the dry rags
of a million mouths to my tongue
as it settles down in its moist nest

ii. morning

a car door slams, an engine groans awake
clouds are cleaning the sky above the street
crisp shadows puzzle the driveway in black and white
magpies choose which eaves should carry walnuts
I wonder why the For Sale sign has suddenly appeared
when we're planting more hedges between us and the forest
all the windows are blinded by gold
two more cars drive away and none return

iii. afternoon

the dog attacks the glass as the girl delivers a flyer
the lawns are growing greener, how green can they get?
my neighbour has a pond and not one fish grows too big for it
cars, boats, RVs, trucks spill out of driveways and garages
I am keeping my flowers in pots as herons sometimes fly overhead
though I am not allowed to keep chickens I feed the birds
the ice cream trucks come less often now
and I don't miss them

iv. evening

the smell of charred meat vaults the fence
we talk about my friend's astronomy app
if you point the iPhone down,
the Southern Cross appears on the screen
it's been beneath our feet all this time
the first star is like a stranger who comes to the door
the sunset so blurry we find ourselves wondering
what's happening out there?

The Spirit of Resistance

You have come to class through the cold
air that wants to get under your clothes
but you won't let it.
You walk into a room so still and dead
even the dry leaf your foot broke on the sidewalk
has more life in it.
In this room, you have no relations.
Here the air loves nothing, not even the virus
that comes out of your lung with a gun.
Every thing in the room is glossed
in plastic or chemical, your feet and elbows
rest on coffin lids of fabric and fossil
boiled and remoleculed.
Your river pebble eyes open
onto chlorine swimming pools.
No sunlight swims here
untubed and unprocessed.
Your cells are not hooks catching the fish of the sun.
Your cells stink in their bags. Time has stopped
washing through your body, rinsing your blades and barbs.
Wildness has been combed out of your tongue.
Your ears are full of machines digging trenches.
Your heart, a frog's deflated belly.
You have no relations. The other beings in the room
are like you, ghosts searching for other ghost faces,
but the rich cloud and compost hair of the underworld
is glued up, cemented over.
You cannot tell if the man in front of the class
is a TV or not. You drift in and out of the room
to turn him off and on.

Once you had a dream that someone
brought a hawk with yellow eyes into this room.
Not an electric dream, but a bone dream.
Backlit wings of a red tailed hawk pressed into a strong wind,
etched a fan-shaped print in your brain.
You dreamt that a witness
had come into the room
to testify that you were still something,
that touch had its warm knots in you.

Mark Tredinnick

Owls

These January nights, I like to walk out late,
When I've shelved my various selves
                            and sent my other lives—
The first and the second and the life after
That—to bed. The world slows
                            to something less than light
Speed after eleven and lets me catch up.
                            I am the last car on the road,

Sloping home late and disconsolate
From a date that didn't quite go
                            where it might have gone.
And tonight, light rain falls, as if from stars,
Which shamble above, the way I amble
                            below, slow-dancing somewhere
Between content and discontent,
                            and two powerful owls,

Cloaked in spindrift, cast their lines out my way
From dark banks. They're flyfishing
                            the night, the new moon for a hook.
There's no bait to take and I don't take it.
Wisdom flies about my head. But not into it.
                            And I would trade almost everything
I know for everything I don't know yet, and the birds do.

Dress Rehearsal

8:00 o'clock. The wind that blew the cloud off the night
                          is still here
      in the morning finishing the job among the regrowth
                                          on the slope.

The sky is the brow of a jenny wren; the rising breeze,
                          her flaring tail.
      The angus on the floodplain paddocks are
                                      in the same place

I left them last night. But someone's shifted the eastern greys
                          a little closer
      to the stream. The forest on the slopes behind the house

Is an orchestra pit of instrument chatter and ribald bird banter
                          before
      the conductor shows. No two of them have the
                                same score. No one

Gives a damn, till the heron flies in very late, her throat a crowd
                          of crotchets
      and river gravel, her heart set on the river.

Reading the Gita Again in Early Spring

I guess it's because I never mastered music that I work so hard
At the music of everything else. The intimate metrics of matter.

I want to tune the world. I want to be played—by time, by trees
And creeks and, yes, by you, as if I were the world's lost lyric.

But with sheet music on the stand and a cello in my arms,
I was the way a boy is with a girl he adores—silenced by awe;

Stupified by longing. All my gestures forced, my fingers
Blind, my moves autistic. But there was—there *always* was—

Another music: the music I long for remembers the world
And finds my self in it when I *bow*, not when I bow, in tuneless

Surrender. When I do anything other than sing, I sing. I find
My Self. Listen to me now: blackbird scratches daylight's back;

Thornbill flies her descant high above the broken glass,
          the thrilling
Mess the frost has made of everything; rufous whistler—
            a faster girl

Than you could ever hope to catch—strikes morning like a match,
And it starts. Two silvereyes, green minstrels, string shocking pink

Villanelles along the limbs of the cherry tree.
         Three magpie larks let loose
Like three tenors unplugged in the plums, which,
          unimpressed, get on

With putting out blossoms into late winter light like Gopi girls
Into Krishna's tent. The unmade clouds are a sleep-stormed bed

The god just rolled out of, a little late, as ever, for work.
                              But work goes on
Anyway, like music; divinity goes on everywhere
                              without the deity,

Unscripted, untenable, unasked for. And very often
                              out of key. What
Happens seems always to have been about to happen—
                              it seems even

To be happening *again*, for the first time this time, here in the
Dreaming present. And so the variegated fairywren, ever so slightly

Overdressed in the rose that drapes like an old and dangerous
Idea across the front porch, is how the god will sound any moment

Now when he gets here. As a young man failing away at the cello,
I was a devotee at the wrong temple, and the eyes of the goddess

Refused to meet mine. Witness is my worship, I see now:
                              another kind
Of play. I am seen by what I see; I am sung, remembering,
                              at my desk;

I am reprised along the forest path, inside the shadowy
                              Darshan of the trees.
My way beyond the world *is* the world—the music of
                              each manifest thing,

Observing its own truth, striking its own note, dressing
                              in no one
Else's drag. And the music that turns *that* music on—
                              and off again, at last.

Katrina Porteous

The Whale

That January, the sea brought us a message –
Monumental, big as a black bus, ribbed,
Rubbery, vulcanized, arched like a bridge,

There it lay one morning – a sperm whale,
Making for another world, and perished.

It looked old as the rock. It was mottled brick-red
And chalked pinkish-white, like a fresco
In a dark church. Its fluke was etched

Delicately greenish-pink; its side
Rose, a black slag-heap, a hill of cinders,
Red oxides, oily residues and clinker.

We were drawn to it. Huddled on the bank-top,
Facing the horizon, hunched against the wind
And cold, we stared and stared at it, in wonder.

Then the sea, with the noise of a great machine,
Rolled its dark bulk towards us and, graceful
As weed, it raised one flipper like a sign;

And the sea heaved; lifted its great weight, light
As a breath, or a gift – Here, take it.

Alice Oswald

Sharpham House

A Letter *(with marginalia and footnotes)*

To Captain Pownoll concerning his Property

> *Philemon Pownoll captured* The Hermione, *a Spanish treasure ship, in 1762 and used his earnings to buy and improve Sharpham. The house was owned by a succession of families after his death and in 1982 was given to the Sharpham Trust.*

Captain, I write in haste this note
About your house. I know your boat,
Under full sail, has turned its prow
Away from us and nothing now
Distracts you as you slide ahead
To the lit dockyards of the dead –   *cow parsley*
Maybe you've almost passed that place
A mile beyond all measured space
Where gentlemen no longer need   *meadow vetchling*
To be defined by gold brocade,
So thin, so infinite you feel,   *yellow flag iris*
Your bare hands barely brush the wheel –
Well, let this letter dispossess
Those hands of their new nothingness,   *red fescue*
For one substantial moment be
Possessed again by property
And suffer for me, please, once more
The weight of walking through a door.

water cress   creeping thistle   ivy-leafed toadflax
Stitchwort

Come in, Captain, let the door close.
Here's nothing but a heap of shoes,
As if your guests, keen to express   *common carder bee*
The paradox of emptiness,
Stood here relinquishing their roots
Until their bodies left their boots.
Don't worry – in an hour or so   *ramshorn snail*
They'll find their feet again and go,
All but one man who stands confused,
Then shuffles off in women's shoes.
Well, Sir, one word about this hall.   *gall wasp*
It is of course your own, but all
The spiders that have pegged their tents
To various lamps and ornaments
Have certain rights here. I can't choose,
In this small hall, whose house is whose,   *ruby tiger moth*
Though its design makes it perhaps
The property of an ellipse.

Slender grass hopper
harlequin ladybird

I'm sorry. Light has taken on
The leasehold of this place, the sun
Lets all sorts in. When morning comes,   *pink purslane*
Joanna squirts and sweeps the rooms
And sometimes finds a muslin moth
Climbing the leaf-print of a cloth   *wild celery*
Or sometimes lightly lifts a blind   *sow thistle*
And there's a crane-fly pressed behind,
Waving its crutches, or a bat
Struggling to fold its corners flat   *scentless mayweed*
And once, she says, a crowd of nuns

Left candles here and baked bean tins.
She says she saw them, stripped of clothes,
Asleep like last year's fruit in rows.
As for the stairwell, when you speak,
A lost, slow-witted ghost speaks back.
You clap, you shout, but nothing moves
The echoes living in its alcoves.

common reed
ribwort plantain   yellow rattle   germander speedwell
large yellow underwing

Let's leave them there and step by step
Ascend this stone one-up-man-ship,
To find at last, on the last floor
The stairs go up and up – the more
You look, the more those spirals rise
On thermals through the canted skies.   *comb-footed spider*
Above this room's another room
And windows, where the white doves come
Rushed in their surplices to sing
Something between grief and breathing,
With neither claims nor consonants,   *ruby-tailed wasp*
Dropped like a password into silence –
It breaks my heart! If only life
Could be so unexposed, so safe
And cradled as the doves imply.
But in the small-print of the sky,
Down all those blue and winding flights,
The Sparrowhawks have feeding rights.

common quaker moth   heart and dart
honey bee
dark arches

It's like, along the Spanish coast,
White sailing ships get tied and tossed,   *reed bunting*
Till English captains, like our own,
Swoop in and pick them to the bone,
Then float away to find a nest
On the dry waves of the South West.
Captain, I love this gated world   *thick-lipped mullet*
Which your brave thieving helped to build,
So that a man might stroll at ease
Under his tolerant friends, the trees,
Or watch his own cows eat across
A paradise of captured grass,   *green dock beetle*
Or find a chair beneath a bough
And write a note, as I do now.
Though even as I speak, a spider
Is putting footnotes on the paper.
Let's go, before the grass begins
To seed itself along the margins…

Perennial rye grass   English scurvy grass

chiff-chaff
    woodland meadow grass   *chiff chaff*

      scented vernal grass

false oat grass

also ragged robin, goose foot and milk maids,
meadow foxtail, marsh thistle, willowherb, ribwort plantain,
   spearthistle and black knapweed,

*nettles and harts-tongue ferns, hogweed, silverweed and several
other small waving figures in the teaming freedom of the fields,*

grasshoppers and the ghosts of dandelions,

red campion, rousing itself like a strong man after sleep,

*comb-footed spiders, yellow dung-flies and all
near-sighted things – click beetles and barnacles*

*and far-sighted ones such as moonlight and sunlight and
the light of human conscience,*

*the mass-produced mud, the orchid peering out from the
underworld, the free-born rain, the dawn, all the durable
materials of winter and the perishable goods of summer
such as birdsong too volatile and subtle to be kept,*

*white rot and carrot fly close to the ground and a crow's
crooked way of walking,*

*ruby-tailed wasps, green dock beetles and a group of shelduck
taking their pupils to the water,*

five doves like washed white gloves,

a sapling uprooted, three or four eggs pale greenish white,

a coffee pot, beige enamel with green edges

*barbed wire and stiff-fingered bracken and fungus
like an old man's ears,*

yellow flag iris, white clover, creeping buttercup, cow parsley,

*a gateless gate in the woods, a rookery, a reed warbler's house
put together swiftly out of straw and the river comes in
and out of the ground floor without asking,*

*a twelfth century heronry with inherited herons and ivy and
other self-seeking things such as the sea
paying its accustomed tithe twice daily,*

two swans still in their wedding clothes and seagulls
owning nothing only open mouths

as well as all transparent things such as floodwater
and new leaves,

shore crabs, thick-lipped mullet, eels, herring gulls, water mint
and slow-motion litter heading south with the tide
and a dog barking at its echo and crowds of
narcissus,

surface water and cess pools and the overflow
from pumps and wells,

a sea-chest covered with cow's hide marked P.P.

plus a cloud of flattering thorn-flowers, the wind working
all morning without obligation of rent or service,

honey bees a billion of them plugging their equipment into
the limes, horse chestnuts, walnuts, even larches a roomful
of teenage trees in light green sleeves now fallen,

solar panels like tilted pools,

electricity flying over the fields on wires,

and desolate people sitting on benches or sliding
on bikes over horizons,

grey squirrels, hares, rabbits, the hand prints of ducks,
the earth annotated by an
otter,

let snowdrops take the slopes, let the cowsheds belong
to themselves, now the whole shore-line is going
going gone to the reeds with rents and quit-rents for
incoming tides, delightful situation, lovely garden
and park and thirty-seven cottages each one lit by the
thin flame of a human, hedge woundwort, chickweed,
smut, violets, spies in the woods, wild blackberries and

*raspberries, a bend in the river with back swimmers,
mirid bugs, common mouse ear, lesser swine cress,
water dropwort, wood avens, not to mention the long
vowels of pigeons and the clipped panic of blackbirds,
the anxiety of the line of flight of the buff-tip swallow,
the green carpet moth, the white ermine, dunbar, treble
lines and large yellow underwing, oak apple, Yorkshire
fog, carrageen, horned wrack, sponge, pignut, flatfish,
little egret, greater stitchwort, war veterans, elm bark
beetles, long-jawed orb web spiders, harvestmen,
poets, palmate newts, vines with hard-worked
knuckles, nuns with oil cloths on their heads, cheese
makers, teenagers, rowers, leeches, greater horseshoe
bats, geese always swearing and leaving their rubbish
in the fields, Siberian willows, Buddhists, historians,
sheep, snow, dock leaves, cancers and traumas, more
rye grass, dog's mercury, fertiliser sacks, a sock, apple
trees, sculptures, dust, microbes, spores, a rusted rake,
a haybale, myself climbing over a stile, a yoghurt pot,
vague feelings, a washed up sandal, two ponies not
wanting to be stroked and badgers eating crisps in the
undergrowth, a goat god, even deer who spring away
full of hydrogen almost too light to stay grounded and
at low tide little mouths open in the mud which sing
such mournful unbreathing songs, there are broken
bottles here and lime kilns, volcanic stuff, eight marble
cupids each one with an instrument, midges, bluebells
and red earth and someone's dinghy now full of
black liquid, the natural idleness of bindweed, lichen,
chickens, and a fleet of tents in point field, one musket
ball lodged in the chest that one is yours that one is
yours, a barn owl, a raven, cloakrooms, cutlery, light
damage and failing paint, strimmers, chainsaws, stars,*

*a German fighter plane bursting into the trance above
the river and about two hundred swimmers setting out
from north quay and*

all these things are written down as yours

but of course

life is not so limited in its pen and ink ...

Contributors

Alec Finlay is a Scottish-born poet and artist based in Newcastle upon Tyne. Finlay has adopted such innovative poetic forms as the mesostic and circle poem. A particular area of interest is wilderness landscape and the natural environment; his current project, *skying*, surveys renewable technologies and landscape (www.skying.co.uk). Previous projects include *the road north*, a collaborative web-based 'word-map' of Scotland (www.theroadnorth.co.uk). Poetry publications include *Mesostic Remedy* (morning star, 2009), *Mesostic Interleaved* (morning star & The University of Edinburgh, 2009), and *Ian Hamilton Finlay: Selections* (ed. Alec Finlay, University of California Press, 2012).

Alice Oswald lives in Devon and is married with three children. *Dart*, her second collection, won the T. S. Eliot Prize in 2002. *Woods etc*, was a Poetry Book Society Choice and was shortlisted for the Forward Prize for Best Collection and the T. S. Eliot Prize. Her latest book is *Memorial* (Faber, 2011). The poem 'Sharpham House' was originally commissioned by the Sharpham Trust to mark their 30th anniversary.

Alistair Peebles grew up in southwest Scotland, studied in Aberdeen and has lived and worked in Orkney since 1985. He is currently engaged in research on the early work of Ian Hamilton Finlay, which he is now pursuing at Northumbria University in Newcastle. The poems presented here were first published in 2011 in *Turning Space,* under his own imprint, Brae Editions.

Allen Tullos is the senior editor of SouthernSpaces.org and a professor of American Studies at Emory University in Atlanta, Georgia. He has most recently published poetry in the *Connecticut Poetry Review* and *Southern Quarterly* and is the author of *Alabama Getaway: The Political Imaginary and the Heart of Dixie* (Univ. of Georgia Press, 2011).

Andrew Forster has published two collections of poetry with Flambard Press, *Fear of Thunder* and *Territory*. *Fear of Thunder* was shortlisted for the Forward Prize for Best First Collection in 2008, and poems from it feature on the AQA GCSE syllabus.

Territory explores the landscape of southwest Scotland, where he then lived. Roncadora Press recently published a pamphlet, *Digging*, a collaboration with the artist Hugh Bryden. He is Literature Officer for the Wordsworth Trust.

Andy Brown's latest poetry book is *The Fool and the Physician*, based on the paintings of Bosch. Recent books include *Goose Music*, with John Burnside, and *Fall of the Rebel Angels: Poems 1996-2006* (all Salt Publishing). His chapbooks including *The Storm Berm* (tall-lighthouse), *The Trust Territory* (Heaventree), and *Of Science* (with David Morley, Worple Press). A selection of his verse appears in *Identity Parade* (Bloodaxe Books, 2010), and his prose poems in *This Line's Not For Turning* (Cinnamon, 2011). He is Director of Creative Writing at Exeter University and was previously an Arvon Centre Director at Totleigh Barton.

Ariel Gordon is a writer based on the Canadian prairies. In spring 2010, Palimpsest Press published her first full-length poetry collection, *Hump*. The chapbook *How to Prepare for Flooding* (JackPine Press), a collaboration with designer Julia Michaud, was launched in fall 2011. When not being bookish, Ariel likes tromping through the woods and taking macro photographs of mushrooms.

Arpine Konyalian Grenier's work has been described as a mosaic of narrative that takes us out of a provincial concentration on life to encompass broader social and geopolitical issues with a decidedly urban and postmodern sensibility. Her latest is a collection of hybrid text titled, *The Concession Stand: Exaptation at the Margins* (Otolith books, 2011).

Ben Smith is studying for a PhD in Creative Writing at Exeter University. His poetry and criticism have appeared in various magazines including *Agenda*, *Acumen*, *The London Magazine*, *Poetry Wales* and *PN Review*.

Cathleen Allyn Conway is originally from Chicago but lives in London. She is a poet, a journalist, and a research student on Sylvia Plath at the University of Greenwich. Her work has appeared in *Magma*, *South Bank Poetry*, *3:AM Magazine*, *Plath*

Profiles, and *Ink Sweat and Tears*. Her first pamphlet, *Static Cling*, was published in April 2012 by Dancing Girl Press.

Catherine Owen is a Vancouver BC writer, the author of nine collections of poetry and one of prose. Her work has won awards, been translated & published in North America, England, Italy, Turkey, Australia, Germany and Korea. In 2001 she completed her Masters' thesis on the ecological poetry of Robinson Jeffers and in 2012 she composed five songs for a Canadian eco-musical called 'Awakening the Green Man'. These poems are from a new manuscript titled *Riven*, lyrics on the Fraser River. Her website is www.catherineowen.org and she runs a blog at blackcrow2.wordpress.com.

Charles Wilkinson's collection of poems came out from Iron Press and a book of his short stories was published by London Magazine Editions. Some of the poems in his 'Marches' sequence have appeared in *Envoi*, *Poetry Wales*, *Staple* and *Tears in the Fence*. His recent work includes an article in *The Reader* on the neglected novelist William Gerhardie and a short story in *Unthology 2* (Unthank Books). He lives in Presteigne, Powys.

Chris McCully was born in Yorkshire, 1958. He lectured at Manchester University 1982-2003, thereafter lecturing part-time at the Vrije Universiteit, Amsterdam and the Rijksuniversiteit, Groningen. Recent books include *Outside* (Two Ravens Press, 2011) and *Selected Poems* (Carcanet, 2011). His study of Irish sea-trout fishing, *Nomads of the Tides*, forthcoming from The Medlar Press in 2013. Chris lives close to the Wadden Sea in the north of the Netherlands and tries to divide his time between university work and writing. www.chrismccully.co.uk

C. J. Allen's poetry has appeared in magazines & anthologies in the UK, USA, Ireland & elsewhere & has regularly been awarded prizes in numerous competitions. His most recent collections are: *A Strange Arrangement: New and Selected Poems* (Leafe Press, 2007) and *Lemonade* (a red ceilings press e-book, 2010, http://issuu.com/theredceilings/docs/lemonade). *Violets* – winner of the Templar Press Short Collection Competition – was published in November 2011, and *At the Oblivion Tea-Rooms* (Nine Arches Press) is due later this year.

David Chorlton has lived in Phoenix since 1978 when he moved from Vienna, Austria, with his wife. Born in Austria, he grew up in Manchester. In his early 20s he went to live in Vienna and from there enjoyed many trips around Europe to enjoy and paint its landscapes and towns. In Arizona he has grown ever more fascinated by the desert and its wildlife, and especially enjoys the mountain ranges of southern Arizona. In 2008, he won the Ronald Wardall Award from Rain Mountain Press for his chapbook *The Lost River*, and in 2009 the Slipstream Chapbook Competition for *From the Age of Miracles*. Other recent poetry collections include *Return to Waking Life* (Main Street Rag Publishing Company), *The Porous Desert* (FutureCycle), and *Waiting for the Quetzal* (March Street Press). *The Taste of Fog* (Rain Mountain Press) is his first work of fiction, and the result of a long-standing interest in Vienna's shadow side.

David Troupes grew up in Massachusetts, holds degrees from the University of Massachusetts at Amherst and the University of Edinburgh, and now lives with his wife in West Yorkshire. His two books of poems, *Parsimony* (2009) and *The Simple Men* (2012) were published by Two Ravens Press. His other work includes the online comic *Buttercup Festival*, publications from Knucker Press, critical work on Ted Hughes, and collaborations with illustrator Laurie Hastings and composer Joel Rust. When he's not writing, drawing or working, he's walking.

dee Hobsbawn-Smith is a chef, poet, writer and educator. She lives in a 100-year-old farmhouse west of Saskatoon. Her fiction, poems and non-fiction have appeared in magazines, newspapers and literary journals in Canada and the USA, including *The Antigonish Review, The Malahat Review, The Windsor Review* and *Gastronomica*. Her new book, *Foodshed: An Edible Alberta Alphabet* is published by TouchWood Editions.

Dilys Rose lives in Edinburgh. She writes mostly fiction and poetry and enjoys creative collaborations with visual artists and composers. She has published ten books, including *Pest Maiden, Lord of Illusions* and *Bodywork*. She is programme director for the new online MSc in Creative Writing at the University of Edinburgh.

Elizabeth Dodd teaches creative writing and literature at Kansas State University. Her newest book is *Horizon's Lens: My Time On the Turning World* (University of Nebraska Press, 2012).

Em Strang is currently studying for a PhD in Ecopoetry at Glasgow University (Dumfries). She has published poems in the *Glasgow Herald* as well as in a number of poetry journals including *Markings, Poetry Scotland, Dark Mountain, Causeway, New Writing Scotland, Ecozon@* and *Southlight*. She lives in Dumfriesshire with her husband and two daughters.

Fiona Russell's MLitt final folio/collection of prose and poetry, *Where Clouds Come To Die*, won a Sir Patrick Geddes Memorial Trust Award in 2010 for the best piece of coursework by a student at a Scottish university following Geddesian principles. Other publications have included Markings, Pushing Out The Boat, and Southlight. She has appeared in three DGAA Poetry Doubles Poetry Doubles series as 'the up-and-coming local poet' reading with a well-known national poet. Fiona has twice read at the Wigtown Spring Book Festival for the University of Glasgow and also at the Autumn Book Festival on DGAA projects and with Crichton Writers. She has had work selected for the DGAA Kinetic Poetry project. Fiona has had several collaborative publications with local poets and artists. Several of these were for local environmental events. Fiona, a founder member of Crichton Writers, a facilitator for local writing groups and for John Muir Awards, lives on the family hill sheep farm with her rescue lurchers.

Frances Presley was born in Derbyshire, of Dutch-Javanese and English parents. She grew up in Lincolnshire and Somerset, and lives in north London. She studied modern literature at the universities of East Anglia and Sussex, and worked as a librarian and, more recently, at the Poetry Library. Publications of poems and prose include *Somerset Letters* (Oasis, 2002), with drawings by Ian Robinson, which explored intersections of community and landscape. The title sequence of *Paravane: new and selected poems, 1996-2003* (Salt, 2004) was a response to 9/11/2001, and the IRA bombsites in London. *Myne: new and selected poems and prose, 1976-2005*, (Shearsman, 2006) takes its title from the old name for Minehead in Somerset. Her last book, *Lines of Sight*,

(Shearsman, 2009), includes 'Stone settings and Longstones', an approach to the Neolithic stone sites on Exmoor, which is part of a multi-media collaboration with Tilla Brading. Presley has written various essays and reviews, especially on innovative British women poets. Her work is included in the anthologies *Infinite Difference* (Shearsman, 2010), and *Ground Aslant: radical landscape poetry* (Shearsman, 2011).

Gerry Loose is a poet, writer (and land-artist) who works primarily with subjects from the natural world, as well as the world of geopolitics. His work is often to be found inscribed on wood and stone in natural landscapes, Parks and Botanic Gardens and galleries as well as on the page. His most recent publications are *Printed on Water, New and Selected Poems* (Shearsman 2007) and *that person Himself* (Shearsman 2009) His awards include: Creative Scotland Award, Kooneen Säätiö Award, and Herman Kesten Award.

Gordon McInnes was born in Glasgow but raised in North-East England. A favourite theme of his is the coast-line of the north of Britain. He has been published in *Gutter, New Writing Scotland, Kenaz* and other magazines. His pamphlet *Sand and Scar* is available from Vision Street Press.

Howard Giskin has taught in the Department of English at Appalachian State University since 1989. He works mainly in the area of World Literature, with particular interest in Asian culture, literature and philosophy, as well as Latin American literature. He has co-edited *An Introduction to Chinese Culture through the Family* (SUNY Press, 2001), and has edited a volume of Chinese folktales (NTC / Contemporary, 1997), as well as written articles on Argentinean writer Jorge Luis Borges, and published poetry. His interests also include the intersection of the sciences and humanities. He has taught in Asia, Africa, Europe and Latin America, and lives with his wife Vicki in Millers Creek, North Carolina.

Ian Seed edits www.shadowtrain.com. His most recent publications are a pamphlet of prose poems, *Threadbare Fables* (Like This Press, 2012) a full-length collection of poetry, *Shifting Registers*

(Shearsman 2011), a longish short story, *Amore mio* (Flax ebooks 2011), and a translation from the Italian poetry of Ivano Fermini, *the straw which comes apart* (Oystercatcher, 2010).

Isabel Galleymore graduated from the University of St Andrews with an MLitt in Creative Writing in 2011. Since then her poems have featured in *Poetry Review*, *Mslexia* and *The Rialto* and she was elected as a Hawthornden Fellow. Most recently Isabel received an AHRC award in Environment and Sustainability for a PhD in Ecopoetics and Pedagogy that she will commence this year.

Jane McKie's first collection, *Morocco Rococo* (Cinnamon Press), was awarded the 2008 Sundial/Scottish Arts Council prize for best first book of 2007. Her other publications include *When the Sun Turns Green* (Polygon, 2009) and *Garden of Bedsteads* (Mariscat, 2011). She won the 2011 Edwin Morgan International Poetry Competition. She currently teaches on the MSc in Creative Writing at the University of Edinburgh.

Jane Joritz-Nakagawa's sixth poetry book, *notational*, was published by Otoliths in June, 2011. Her 2012 publications include a poetry broadside, *blank notes*, with Country Valley Press, and two poetry chapbooks, *flux of measure* and *season of flux*, with quarter after press. Jane lives in Japan. Email is welcome at <janenakagawa@yahoo.com>.

Jane Routh is a poet and photographer who manages woodlands and a flock of geese in the Forest of Bowland, North Lancashire, where she has lived for the last forty years. Before poetry claimed all her creative energies, Jane's photographs were exhibited in group and solo shows in the north and midlands. Since then, she's published three full collections of poems and has been shortlisted for a Forward prize and received a PBS recommendation, as well as publishing pamphlets and anthologised selections, including creative non-fiction. She won the Academi Cardiff International Poetry Competition in 2009, and the Strokestown International Poetry Competition in 2011.

Jennifer Wallace teaches at the Maryland Institute College of Art in Baltimore, Maryland. She is a poetry editor at *The Cortland Review* and a founding editor of Toadlily Press. Her chapbook, *Minor Heaven*, appears in *Desire Path* (Toadlily Press, 2005). In 2009 she directed a short documentary, *Inter : View, A Conversation About Nature and the City*. Her photographs have been exhibited at the Baltimore Museum of Art and at the Maryland Institute College of Art. She has written essays for exhibition catalogs and literary magazines; her poems appear in numerous journals and anthologies. A book of poems and photographs, *It Can Be Solved by Walking*, is due out from CityLit Press in April 2012.

Jim Carruth was born in Johnstone and grew up on his family's farm near Kilbarchan. His first collection *Bovine Pastoral* was published in 2004. Since then he has brought out a further four collections and an illustrated fable. In 2009 he was awarded a Robert Louis Stevenson Fellowship and was the winner of the James McCash poetry competition. His work was showcased in *Oxford Poets 2010* and his most recent collection *Working the Hill* came out in 2011.

John Glenday's first collection *The Apple Ghost* won a Scottish Arts Council Book Award and his second, *Undark*, was a Poetry Book Society Recommendation. His most recent collection *Grain* (Picador, 2009) is also a Poetry Book Society Recommendation and was shortlisted for both the Ted Hughes Award and the Griffin Poetry Prize. He was a judge for the 2011 National Poetry Competition. In 1990/91 he was appointed Scottish/Canadian Exchange Fellow, based at the University of Alberta. The poem 'Only a leaf for a sail' first appeared online in '7 short sails' – http://studiolog.heriot-toun.co.uk/7sails/7sails_sail_06.php]

John Kinsella's most recent volume of poetry is *Armour* (Picador, 2011). His book of poetry translations and versions, *The Jaguar's Dream* (Herla/Alma Books), has just been released. His *Activist Poetics: Anarchy in the Avon Valley* (Liverpool) was published in 2010. He is a Fellow of Churchill College, Cambridge University, and a Professorial Research Fellow at the University of Western Australia.

Jorie Graham was born in New York City in 1950, the daughter of a journalist and a sculptor. She was raised in Rome, Italy and educated in French schools. She studied philosophy at the

Sorbonne in Paris before attending New York University as an undergraduate, where she studied filmmaking. She received an MFA in poetry from the University of Iowa. Graham is the author of numerous collections of poetry, most recently *Place* (Ecco, 2012), *Sea Change* (Ecco, 2008), *Never* (2002), *Swarm* (2000), and *The Dream of the Unified Field: Selected Poems 1974-1994*, which won the 1996 Pulitzer Prize for Poetry. Graham has also edited two anthologies, *Earth Took of Earth: 100 Great Poems of the English Language* (1996) and *The Best American Poetry 1990*. Her many honors include a John D. and Catherine T. MacArthur Fellowship and the Morton Dauwen Zabel Award from The American Academy and Institute of Arts and Letters. She has taught at the University of Iowa Writers' Workshop and is currently the Boylston Professor of Rhetoric and Oratory at Harvard University. She served as a Chancellor of The Academy of American Poets from 1997 to 2003. www.joriegraham.com

Jos Smith has recently completed his PhD at the University of Exeter, an archipelagic perspective on recent British and Irish nature writing. He hopes to go on to lecture and research in literature and the rise of the environmental movement in Britain and Ireland. He is currently working on his first collection of poetry and a book on walking in the south of England.

Kathleen Jones' first pamphlet of poetry, *Unwritten Lives*, won the Redbeck Press pamphlet award and her first collection, *Not Saying Goodbye at Gate 21* (Templar Poetry, November 2011) was joint winner of the Straid Award. Kathleen also writes biographies, including a life of Christina Rossetti, *Learning not to be First* (OUP) and *A Passionate Sisterhood – the sisters, wives and daughters of Wordsworth, Coleridge and Southey* (Virago). *Katherine Mansfield: The Story-Teller*, was published in 2011 by Penguin and EUP. Kathleen lives in Cumbria, has taught creative writing in a number of universities and is currently a Royal Literary Fund Fellow.

Katrina Porteous lives on the Northumberland coast and her work explores the human and natural history of that area; in particular, the culture of the inshore fishing community. She is best known for her long poems for BBC Radio, which include: *Horse*, *The Refuge Box*, *Dunstanburgh*, *Longshore Drift* and *An*

Ill Wind. Her books include: *The Lost Music* (Bloodaxe 1996) and *The Blue Lonnen* (Jardine 2007). She is an ambassador for the creative alliance New Networks for Nature. 'The Whale' was first broadcast on BBC Radio 3's *The Verb*, November 2010.

Les Murray was born in 1938 and grew up on a dairy farm at Bunyah on the north coast of New South Wales, where he still lives. Carcanet publish his *Collected Poems* and his *New Selected Poems* (2012), as well as his individual collections. Blake Morrison, writing in the *Independent on Sunday*, called Murray 'one of the finest poets writing in English today, one of the super league which includes Seamus Heaney, Derek Walcott and Joseph Brodsky'. In 2007, Dan Chiasson wrote in *The New Yorker* that he is 'now routinely mentioned among the three or four leading English-language poets'. In 1996 Murray won the TS Eliot Award for *Subhuman Redneck Poems*, and in June 1999 he was awarded The Queen's Gold Medal for Poetry at Buckingham Palace, an honour that was recommended by the late Poet Laureate Ted Hughes.

Mario Petrucci's work, 'Reminiscent of e.e. cummings at his best', aspires to 'Poetry on a geological scale' (*Verse*). *Heavy Water: a poem for Chernobyl* (Enitharmon, 2004) secured the Daily Telegraph/ Arvon Prize and 'inflicts ... the finest sort of shock ... to the conscience, to the soul' (*Poetry London*). *i tulips* (Enitharmon, 2010) takes its name from his vast Anglo-American sequence of 1111 poems, hailed by the Poetry Book Society as 'modernist marvels'. A PhD physicist and ecologist, Mario is intensely active at the literature-ecology-science membrane, generating groundbreaking educational resources and poetry that combines issues of searing social, linguistic and personal relevance with innovation and humanity. www.mariopetrucci.com

Mark Goodwin lives and works as a community poet in Leicestershire. He has two collections with Shearsman, *Else* (2008) and *Back of A Vast* (2010); and a collection called *Shod* (2010), with Nine Arches Press, which won the first East Midlands Book Award. Mark is included in Shearsman's anthology, *The Ground Aslant, Radical Landscape Poetry* (2010) and Longbarrow Press's *The Footing* (2012), an anthology of walking poetry. Mark is a climber, walker, balancer, stroller & experiencer of place.

Mark Tredinnick has been described as 'one of our great poets of place—not just of geographic place, but of the spiritual and moral landscape as well' (Judy Beveridge). The winner of many Australian poetry awards, including the Blake and Newcastle Prizes, Tredinnick won the Montreal International Poetry Prize in 2011 and the Cardiff Poetry Prize in 2012. Mark's eleven works of poetry and prose include *Fire Diary* (winner of the WA Premier's Book Award), *The Blue Plateau* (shortlisted for the Prime Minister's Literary Awards, winner of the Queensland Premier's Literary Award), *The Little Red Writing Book*, *The Land's Wild Music* and *Australia's Wild Weather*. His poems and essays are widely published in Australia, the UK and the United States. With Kate Rigby, Mark founded the Association for Literature and the Environment–ANZ, and he's a member of Kangaloon, a fellowship of Australian poets, scholars and activists, working to awaken beautiful, intelligent, and enduring responses to species loss, climate change and the impoverishment of life. He lives with his family on the Wingecarribee River, southwest of Sydney.

Meg Bateman lectures in literature and philosophy at Sabhal Mòr Ostaig, University of the Highlands and Islands. She was born in Edinburgh in 1959, and learnt Gaelic in South Uist and the University of Aberdeen where she taught for many years. She has translated and co-edited anthologies of Gaelic medieval, 17th-century and religious verse. Her own poetry is included in numerous anthologies, and in two collections, *Aotromachd/ Lightness* and *Soirbheas/ Fair Wind*, which were short-listed for the Scottish Book of the Year award in 1997 and 2007.

Nancy Holmes is a Canadian poet who has published four books of poetry, most recently *Mandorla* with Ronsdale Press (2005). A fifth book of poetry, forthcoming from Ronsdale Press, will be called *The Flicker Tree*. Nancy edited the anthology *Open Wide a Wilderness: Canadian Nature Poems* (2009) for Wilfrid Laurier University Press, and has had fiction and poetry published in many literary journals.

Paul Lindholdt was raised in Seattle. He has worked as a longshoreman, a Teamster who processed seafood, an industrial waste recycler, and a builder – stories that come into his 2011

University of Iowa essay collection *In Earshot of Water*. Professor of English at Eastern Washington University, he studies American literature and culture through the lenses of environmental politics. He works in history, journalism, literature, and online learning.

Paul Kingsnorth is the author of *Kidland, and Other Poems* (Salmon, 2011.) His poetry has been published in a wide and eclectic selection of publications over the last two decades, and his awards include BBC Wildlife Poet of the Year, and the 2012 Wenlock Poetry Prize. Paul is also the co-founder and director of the Dark Mountain Project, a cultural focus point for writers and artists who aim to question the stories our civilisation tells about itself. www.paulkingsnorth.net

Pippa Little is Scots but lives in Northumberland. *Overwintering* (Oxford Poets/Carcanet) is published in October 2012. Her work has appeared in many anthologies and magazines and she has co-edited two anthologies for Virago. She is a founding member of the writers' workshop Carte Blanche.

Rody Gorman was born in Dublin in 1960 and now lives in the Isle of Skye. He has published several poetry collections in English, Irish and Scottish Gaelic. His selected poems in Irish and Scottish Gaelic, *Chernilo*, were published in 2006. He has worked as writing fellow at Sabhal Mòr Ostaig, University College Cork and the University of Manitoba and is editor of the annual Irish and Scottish Gaelic poetry anthology *An Guth*.

Roger Mitchell is the author of eleven books of poetry, among them *Lemon Peeled the Moment Before: New and Selected Poems* (2008). Two previous books include *Half/Mask* (2007) and *Delicate Bait*, which Charles Simic chose for the Akron Prize, in 2003. Other recognition for his writing includes two fellowships each from the National Endowment for the Arts and the Indiana Arts Commission and one from the New York Foundation for the Arts. He lives in mountains of northern New York.

Rupert M. Loydell is Senior Lecturer in English with Creative Writing at University College Falmouth, and the editor of *Stride* and *With* magazines. He is the author of several collections of poetry, including the recent *Wildlife* from Shearsman, and *A Music Box of Snakes*, co-authored with Peter Gillies, from Knives, Forks & Spoons Press. He edited *Smartarse* for Knives Forks & Spoons Press, *From Hepworth's Garden Out: poems about painters and St. Ives* for Shearsman, and *Troubles Swapped for Something Fresh, an anthology of manifestos and unmanifestos*, for Salt. He lives in a creekside village with his family and far too many CDs and books.

Ruth Padel's latest book is *The Mara Crossing*, an exploration in poetry and prose of migration in cells, animals, birds, people and souls. Her works include *Where the Serpent Lives*, a novel featuring tropical zoology and wildlife crime, and *Tigers in Red Weather* on tiger conservation. Poetry collections include *Darwin – A Life in Poems* and *The Soho Leopard*. She is a Council Member of the Zoological Society of London which spear-heads conservation of wild animals and their habitats across the globe. See http://www.ruthpadel.com/

Sharon Black is originally from Glasgow but now lives in the Cévennes mountains of southern France. She is a regular visitor to the west coast of Scotland and much of her poetry is inspired by the landscapes of her homeland and of her adopted land. Her work has been published widely and she won The Frogmore Poetry Prize 2011. Her first full poetry collection, *To Know Bedrock*, was published by Pindrop Press in 2011. www.sharonblack.co.uk

Susan Richardson is a poet, performer and educator based in Wales. Her most recent poetry collection, *Where the Air is Rarefied* (Cinnamon Press, 2011), is a collaboration with a printmaker on a range of environmental and mythological themes relating to the Far North. Susan regularly performs her work at literary and green festivals throughout the UK and is one of the resident poets on BBC Radio 4's Saturday Live. She has been poet-in-residence for BBC 2's coverage of the Chelsea Flower Show and was recently invited to become a Fellow of the International League of Conservation Writers. www.susanrichardsonwriter.co.uk

Susan Rowland is Core Faculty at Pacifica Graduate Institute and formerly Professor of English and Jungian Studies at the University of Greenwich UK. Specializing in ecocriticism, Jung, gender and literary theory, her books include *Jung: A Feminist Revision* (2002), *Jung as a Writer* (2005) and *C.G. Jung in the Humanities* (2010). Her new book is *The Ecocritical Psyche: Literature, Complexity Evolution and Jung* (2012). From 2003-6 Susan was the founding chair of the International Association for Jungian Studies. She current teaches on a hybrid Jungian/Archetypal Studies program and on an MA in Engaged Humanities and the Creative life at Pacifica.

Susie Patlove was a 2008 finalist for a Massachusetts Cultural Council award and a winner of the Poet's Seat Poetry Prize. Her work as appeared on NPR's *The Writer's Almanac* and in Ted Kooser's column *American Life in Poetry*. She has several poems in the new anthology *Morning Song*, from St. Martin's Press, 2011. Her book, *Quickening*, was published by Slate Roof Press in 2007. She lives with her husband in western Massachusetts.

Terry Jones won 1st prize for poetry in the 2011 Bridport competition, and in 2012 won 1st prize in the Sentinel Annual Poetry Competition. Originally from Bradford, he now lives and works in Carlisle. A keen fell walker, he appreciates the proximity of the Lake District. Married with three grown-up children, he has recently left a career as lecturer in English Literature for independent work as a private tutor and freelance writer. Terry won first prize in the 2001 Ottakars/Observer national poetry competition and has twice been highly commended in the Mirehouse competition. His poems have been published in *Poetry Review, Agenda, The Rialto, The London Magazine, Magma, Iota, Envoi, the Dark Horse, Pennine Platform, Orbis* and others. His first short collection, *Furious Resonance*, was published in 2011 by Poetry Salzburg. http://terryjonespoetry.weebly.com/

Two Ravens Press is the most remote literary publisher in the UK, operating from a working croft by the sea, right at the end of the most westerly road on the Isle of Lewis in the Outer Hebrides. Our approach to publishing is as radical as our location: Two Ravens Press is run by two writers with a passion for language and for books that are nonformulaic and that take risks. Visit our website for comprehensive information on all of our books and authors:

www.tworavenspress.com

EarthLines is a lavishly illustrated, full-colour A4-sized quarterly magazine of 64 pages, dedicated to high quality writing on nature, place and the environment. Our focus is on writing which explores the relationship between people and the natural world, and encourages reconnection. We want to help forge a new ecoliterature that is truly responsive to, and that deeply and meaningfully engages with, the challenges we face. That doesn't just acknowledge, but that actively embraces all the contradictions and discomforts inherent in our relationship with the natural world – those contradictions which surface in all of our genuine attempts to reconnect. The first year's issues will include Jay Griffiths, John Lister-Kaye, Hugh Warwick, Andrew Greig, Sara Maitland, John Kinsella, Carry Akroyd, Jeremy Mynott, Jorie Graham and Margaret Elphinstone, as well as many other well-known, new and emerging writers.

'*EarthLines* is a deeply intelligent publication, sensitive to nature and culture, and it has what is perhaps the greatest quality in a magazine: curiosity.' JAY GRIFFITHS

'What a fine thing you've made in the magazine and the culture that goes with it: a real point of convergence for many thought-tributaries and philosophical paths.' ROBERT MACFARLANE

- Visit the *EarthLines* website to find out more and to subscribe.
- Read our blog at http://earthlinesmagazine.wordpress.com
- Join us on Facebook & Twitter – just search for 'EarthLines'

www.earthlines.org.uk